Homeschooling
the *Challenging*
Child

A Practical Guide

Christine M. Field

B&H
PUBLISHING GROUP

Nashville, Tennessee

© 2005 by Christine Field
All rights reserved.
Printed in the United States of America.

ISBN: 978-0-8054-3078-3

Published by B&H Publishing Group,
Nashville, Tennessee

Dewey Decimal Classification: 371.042
Subject Heading: HOME SCHOOLING

4 5 6 7 8 9 10 11 12 13   14 13 12 11 10 09

Homeschooling
the *Challenging*
Child

Dedication

I have so many people to thank and recognize. First of all, this book is dedicated to the parents of challenging children. May you persevere in the work the Lord has given you.

A special dedication also goes to Gena Suarez and *The Old Schoolhouse Magazine*. Thank you for opening my eyes to a new area of ministry and for giving me encouragement and a forum for sharing my struggles and successes.

Thank you to the parents who answered a lengthy survey for this book. Your ideas and insights are at the heart of this work.

Thank you to Sharon Carlson, who has taught me so much.

A special thank you to my husband and children, who teach me new lessons on a daily basis.

May you, the reader, be encouraged and enlightened by what you read here, and may the words and thoughts I share bring glory to God.

Disclaimer

I am not a certified teacher. I'm just a mom sharing what I have gleaned along the way in my homeschooling journey. What is written is not intended to diagnose or treat any disorder.

Not every disorder or approach is covered. To do so would turn this into a multivolume special-needs treatise. My intent is to give parents exposure to areas of concern and to point them to resources for further consideration.

Although I am a licensed attorney in the state of Illinois, nothing herein is to be construed as legal advice; it is intended for educational purposes only.

—Christine Field
Wheaton, Illinois

Contents

Introduction

Do you have a challenging child—or two, or more? Maybe they have had an official diagnosis, like ADHD or LD. Or maybe you are still trying to determine the cause of your child's challenges.

Maybe I can help you.

My husband and I started our homeschooling journey with some trepidation, but also with the confidence that we would eventually get the hang of it. After lots of normal trial and error, we hit our homeschooling stride. Our first two kids were good readers and excited learners. Teaching them was effortless and joyous.

My confidence level was so high that I even had the audacity to write books about my experience. I wanted to share my success with others, and the Lord allowed me the forum and the medium through which to do so.

Little did I know the challenges that lay ahead!

Our third child was difficult to raise from the beginning. When she arrived in our home via adoption at five months of age, she had a large bald spot on the back of her head—an indication that she had been allowed to lie alone for much of those first few months. Still, we believed that love could conquer all, so we set about to fill up her love quotient.

She blossomed into a sweet toddler, then zoomed into difficulty in the preschool years. She presented discipline and behavioral issues that challenged us. When she turned "school age," we sought professional help. We first learned that she had ADHD, and later received the professional opinion that she also had a learning disability.

Those few years shook our confidence and caused us to rely even more strongly on the Lord. We learned many lessons about the real heart of homeschooling as well as about ourselves.

Then came our son—child number four. After handling three sweet girls with some success, we asked the Lord for a boy. He also arrived via adoption at five months of age with lots of self-confidence, a loving heart, and a little boy's enthusiasm! Having a little boy in the house after so many years of solely girls was like driving a Mack truck into the living room! No, I don't think he is hyperactive. I believe he is a normal, healthy, curious boy who daily amazes me with his capacity for wonder! However, many who meet him believe he is hyperactive, and some of the behavior strategies we use with him are the same as for ADHD kids.

Webster's dictionary defines a *challenge* as "anything, as a demanding task, that calls for special effort or dedication."[1] Raising children in itself is a demanding task, requiring the best of our energy and creativity. But what happens when it does not go smoothly? Are you a parent for whom the bumps in the road of parenting and homeschooling seem insurmountable? Your task will take that special effort and dedication, but I assure you that it can be done. There are creative solutions to the challenges you face.

A challenging child may be the strong-willed child. Maybe you have tried all the current strategies to manage their behavior and are at the end of your homeschooling rope. Day-to-day life with a strong-willed child is difficult enough, but when homeschooling is added to the mix, the challenge may become overwhelming. Rest assured that many other parents have hometaught these tough kids and have lived to tell about it. There are proven strategies and approaches to bring out the best in these children.

A challenging child may be the one whose personality does not mesh with yours. She rubs you the wrong way, every day, all day. Can this relationship grow closer? I believe so. Even a strained, distant parent-child relationship can experience the redemptive healing of Christ's touch. You must simply be willing and prayerful, and equip yourself with knowledge about personality types and what motivates each.

I don't like labels, but I have learned not to fear them. Getting a professional diagnosis can be a blessing because it may explain years of struggle and resolve doubts about your ability to parent the challenging child. I also will discuss when professional intervention is desirable and how to begin to look for help.

Homeschooling is tough, hard work and requires large doses of patience. We live in a society obsessed with speed and immediacy. We want fast food, fast service, and drive-through answers. Unraveling the puzzle of your challenging child involves tenacity. You'll need to persevere in spite of what appears to be overwhelming odds. Searching for answers involves courage as you take risks to try a different approach to helping your child.

Are you facing extra challenges beyond how to teach phonics? Let me share my experiences as well as the collective experiences of other homeschooling moms who teach challenging children. It can be done—and done well!

Courage is fear that has said its prayers.
—Anonymous

CHAPTER ONE

What's Your Challenge?

When Homeschooling Does Not Go Smoothly

> *Success is the ability to go from*
> *failure to failure without losing*
> *your enthusiasm.*
>
> —Winston Churchill

Something was very wrong. Despite two years of intensive phonics, my daughter still laboriously sounded out each letter, often mistaking one for another. By the time she reached the end of a sentence, she was so exhausted from her effort that she did not remember the point of the passage. For example, she would read the word *ball* in the second line but could not remember the same word in the fourth line.

Yet there were many wonderful, positive aspects of her development. She could tell elaborate stories with twists and turns and delightful predicaments. Sometimes I would write them down and read them back to her, much to her delight.

In hands-on activities, like those of science and history, she could recall and narrate much of what was covered, and she displayed a real depth of understanding.

Except on a bad day. On a bad day her memory was extremely challenged, and she was highly distractible. One fine winter day she sat looking out the window at the lightly drifting snow, crying her eyes out. When I asked her what was wrong, she said the snowflakes were "bothering her," keeping her from doing her math.

We became caught up in a cycle of failure and negativity. Because I was blind to what was really going on, I characterized all her difficulty as an issue of character and discipline. If she wasn't following instructions, I disciplined her to build the character of obedience. If she couldn't keep focused on her studies, I disciplined her to build the character of self-control. I was so consumed with disciplining her and building her character that I lost sight of the fact that she was a unique, wonderful creation of the Living God.

After one incident of a supposed character lapse, I spanked her. As was often my practice, I followed the spanking with a prayer that went something like, "Dear Jesus, please help Gracie to obey." Hardly skipping a beat, my precious child prayed, "Dear Jesus, please help Mommy to not be so mean."

Was I being mean? I didn't think so. My husband and I looked at this as another chapter of baby Boot Camp, our playful name for times of intense training of the children. When things were getting slack or attitudes were slipping, we would enter into a training time where we focused most of our time and energy on the issues at hand. However, it seemed that this particular child was in perpetual baby Boot Camp!

When there is more than one child in the family, it is common to play the comparison game. My two older children learned to read easily and effortlessly—when they were ready. After my first child, I had learned to wait for readiness. Back then, as a new I've-got-something-to-prove homeschooling mom, I had tried to teach my first daughter to read at two and a half. She wasn't interested. I tried again at three and a half; she still had no interest. I tried at four and a half—she humored me a little but still wasn't ready. By about five and a half she pretty much taught herself. My second child, on the other hand, practically came out of the womb reading. These first two children were also strong in their academic work and could concentrate when it was required (they could also play and goof around with the best of them when they weren't working).

Then along came this third, challenging child. Parenting her added incredible strain to our little family. Every step of the day was a battle. Whether it was getting her to pick up her socks or pick up a reading book, she was ready for a fight. It was exhausting, and my other children often felt neglected.

In my heart I wanted to believe that she was just going through a "phase" or an interminably long growth spurt. Parents often use this explanation to console themselves when their child's behavior perplexes or annoys them. It is comforting to think that something is a phase because it implies that it will someday come to an end. I desperately wanted to believe this. It calmed my fears about her behavior—the tantrums, the moodiness, and the oppositional behavior. As for her intellectual development, I reasoned that she was on her own timetable. If it was an issue of readiness, I felt I could wait graciously for maturity. What I could not fathom was the forgetfulness, the moodiness, and the tantrums.

My husband and I began piecing the puzzle together with observation and research. We sought creative answers to troubling questions, beginning with our own meticulous observations. Armed with this detailed information, we then sought a two-pronged evaluation.

First of all, at the end of her second grade year of homeschooling, we contacted our local school district and requested a complete evaluation for learning disabilities. There is a divergence of opinion among home-schoolers as to the wisdom of this practice. The Home School Legal Defense Association (HSLDA), for example, is against any type of public school intervention. Others advise parents to pursue a private (and potentially costly) evaluation. We, however, felt confident going to the public school because we knew many of the professionals in our school district. In addition, we were firmly aware of our legal right to do whatever we wished with their findings. We could follow their recommendations and accept proffered services, or dismiss them and seek our own path. (The process to pursue a formal evaluation will be completely covered in chapter 10.)

Why not wait for readiness? Dyslexia expert Dr. Sally Shaywitz writes:

> The apparent large-scale underidentification of reading-disabled children is particularly worrisome because even when school identification takes place it occurs relatively late—often past the optimal age for intervention. Dyslexic children are generally in the third grade or above when they are first identified by their schools; reading disabilities diagnosed after third grade are much more difficult to remediate. The brain is much more plastic in younger children and potentially more malleable for the rerouting of neural circuits. Moreover, once a child falls behind he must make up thousands of unread words to catch up to his peers who are continuing to move ahead. Equally important, once a pattern of reading failure sets in, many children become defeated, lose interest in reading, and develop what often evolves into a lifelong loss of their own sense of self-worth.[1]

After a medical and optical screening, we pursued the second prong of our evaluative process—an extensive evaluation by a private child psychologist for ADHD. This entailed a lengthy questionnaire completed independently by both my husband and myself, two office visits for our daughter, and two office visits for us. At the end of the process, we felt this psychologist had an accurate view of our family life.

In the final analysis, our daughter was deemed to be a fairly routine case of both LD (Learning Disabled) and ADHD (Attention-Deficit/Hyperactivity Disorder). Although she did not exhibit the hyperactive component of ADHD, we learned that there is an equally powerful spectrum of the disorder characterized by inattentiveness, moodiness, and lower energy behavior.

Armed with this information we implemented some creative solutions, and now our daughter is flourishing! We wish we had grasped the bigger picture when we first experienced problems. It is my prayer that this book will be a part of that bigger picture for you in your struggle.

So, what about you? What does your challenge look like?

Carrie in Arizona realized the depth of her situation when her son experienced "emotional outbursts that were inappropriately timed and a vast inability to sit still." This led her on a journey to seek her own family's solutions.

Deborah from California noticed that her son would act very frustrated and angry when he could not accomplish things. It was not typical anger, but seemed so out of the ordinary that it alerted her to some deeper issues.

Kris in Illinois knew early on that her daughter had auditory processing issues because she was not talking at the age of two and had trouble understanding what people said to her. With this early awareness, Kris sought help, and her daughter is faring well with continued intervention.

Karen was first directed to her son's challenge when she realized he had no interest in anything language-related. "We tend to like to do the things we can do well," she observes, "and avoid the things we don't do well." If your child has an intense aversion to reading or math or some other pursuit, it may be attributable to the fact that they are not processing that information well.

Sometimes it is necessary to challenge an "official diagnosis." Sherri's son was referred for testing by his first grade teacher. "The school quickly labeled it ADHD and suggested Ritalin right away," she shared in a survey for this book. But Sherri was not satisfied with that dismissive diagnosis. She continued her own research and determined that her son had central auditory processing difficulties. She concludes, "It was not ADHD and Ritalin would not have helped him."

Perhaps you are the parent of a child who is challenging you with her behavior. Learning is not an issue, but you cannot teach a child who will not listen to you. Deborah from California shared my experience, saying of her daughter, "She's been a challenge since she was born!" If discipline is your challenge, take heart because there are solutions.

Another mom I know is very happy with workbooks and filling in blanks. Her son, however, is a classic kinesthetic learner. She struggles with meshing her teaching style with her child's learning style. This can be the source of tremendous frustration for the homeschooler. Debbie in Texas is a wise woman who has learned to work *with* her child's bent and not against it. Here is her story:

> I first became aware of my child's differences when one of his teachers in "Mother's Day Out" told me that while every one of his friends would sit and color or glue, he refused to do these things. He might do just enough to please his teachers, but no more. So, I began to try these activities at home. I would ask him to color or draw, but he wanted no part of it. The way I handled this was to completely quit trying to engage him in "school." After I accepted the fact that he was not interested in the traditional school-type activities, the pressure was off of both of us and he began to learn!

Both the parents' and child's personality style and type are significant factors. In my own home, I am a driven, strong personality. I must remember that control and accomplishments are not the goal for every human! There are people who are content to seek peace and to smell the roses along the way. The way to motivate their type of personality will differ greatly from another personality type.

In addition to uncovering some personality and discipline strategies, our focus in the remainder of this book will be mostly on learning issues, not physical issues. A child who is blind, deaf, or otherwise physically handicapped is well beyond the scope of this book, as is Down Syndrome or other severe handicaps. This volume is written for the homeschooling family who is experiencing learning roadblocks and is seeking knowledge and guidance to navigate them.

Is Homeschooling Legal?

As an attorney, I often am called upon to answer questions about various aspects of the legality of homeschooling. Plain and simple, under the protection of the First and Fourteenth Amendments of the Constitution, you have the same legal right to homeschool your learning-challenged child as you do any other child. Some states may require more accountability from you, and their regulations may be more stringent. It is a good idea to research your state law thoroughly before you begin home-schooling *any* child. You can check your state's requirements by contacting your local state or county board of education or the Home School Legal Defense Association (see resources section).

In homeschooling circles, you may hear the admonition to steer clear of accepting evaluations or services through the public school district. If you choose to avail yourself of special services through the school district, you may be subject to subtle or overt pressure to enroll your child full-time. Rest assured, you are completely within your rights to homeschool him and say a polite "no, thank you" to their suggestions. In my case, we were able to work out an extremely productive and satisfying arrangement for tutoring that has been an enormous blessing for us. Not every family is so fortunate.

If you decide to approach the public school for assistance, be advised that your own attitude and approach will help determine the level of satis-faction you feel at their response. Some parents storm into the principal's office and demand that they receive special services because, after all, they are taxpayers and their homeschooled children don't receive any benefit from their heavy tax burden. Such an attitude will only alienate the school staff and may put you further away from your goal—that of finding an appropriate diagnosis and approach for your child. It is better to use a calm and gentle approach and express appreciation for their assistance and cooperation. The old adage that you can catch more flies with honey than vinegar applies here. The homeschooler who wishes to be treated with respect by school authorities often must be the first to extend that respect.

Is Homeschooling Best?

As parents of children, challenged or not, we want the best for them. All children need love and support, and a challenging child's needs—both emotional and academic—can be far more intense.

Children who learn or act differently may experience self-confidence and self-esteem issues as they continue to notice their differences. While homeschooling is not the answer for everyone, it can shelter your child from some destructive situations. If your child is already in the special education system, bringing him home also may bring healing for damaged emotions. One mom noted that she was in special education when she was a child. Walking to the resource room while the other children remained in the regular classroom was lonely and humiliating. Homeschooling her child was her answer to spare her child that feeling of humiliation she felt under those circumstances.

Children also are spared the brunt of comparison and competition that is rampant in the classroom. Homeschooling allows us to practice selective socialization, apart from the pain and ridicule of school. We can help our children nurture friendships that are God-honoring and respecting of individual differences.

Most of us, unless we ourselves were homeschooled, have this notion in our minds of the public school experience: lines of neatly arranged desks with children sitting still, listening intently to the teacher and being actively and busily engaged (at varying levels) in the process of "being educated." That, however, may not be reality for your child with a learning challenge.

Their brain is telling them, "Move! Jump! Twist! Turn!" All of their energy is being expended toward that goal. Their brain may be nearly constantly engaged in a rapid-fire mode with mixed, garbled messages—much like a person talking to another person on a walkie-talkie, but on different frequencies. A message comes through, but it is all static noise. Or, the words are understandable, but there are several people talking on the same frequency.

Adjustments need to be made. Think about the old black-and-white television sets that had horizontal and vertical controls to get the picture clearer. Often it took only a slight turn of either of the knobs to get the picture to stop rolling or to take out the vertical or horizontal lines that distorted the true picture. Similarly, making an adjustment in your child's learning environment or your teaching approach may be the key to him having a clear picture. But it takes time and one-on-one attention.

A classic classroom environment with perfectly aligned student desks simply can't give your child the one-on-one attention that is possible in the home. If your child is in school and struggling, consider how much time you spend helping with homework. Have you ever wondered why all the work can't be completed during the school day? Often it is because the child needs additional one-on-one time or practice with a concept. When you homeschool, you eliminate homework because it's all "home work"! If you have helped a tired, cranky, challenging child with homework, rest assured that you will be able to handle homeschooling this child.

Consider also the tremendous benefit of flexibility. You can strengthen the weaknesses and teach to the strengths (a maxim that will be more fully fleshed out in chapter 9 when we talk about planning your program). In addition, you can use materials on many grade levels instead of learning lockstep with the rest of a school. For example, many of us have children who are at one grade level in math and at a completely different grade level in language arts. In the homeschool setting, children experience no stigma or shame, as they use materials and instruction that are appropriate for their abilities. Your schooling environment and program can be perfectly tailored to meet the individual needs of your child.

In the home, you can also exercise greater control over the physical environment. Consider the child with dietary restrictions who daily visits the school cafeteria only to be bombarded with the sights and smells of delicacies (often processed foods) that, if ingested, would send his behavior and concentration into a nosedive. At home a child's diet can be monitored, and other aspects of the environment also can be modified to deal with physical distractions.

Is homeschooling the right alternative for your challenging child? Consider this: homeschooling also can provide you with time and energy to work on your relationship with your child and give you the chance to teach critical life skills, which often have little to do with academics. As parents, our goal is to launch our children out of the home as productive, God-honoring husbands, wives, fathers, mothers, and workers in the workplace.

It can afford you the opportunity to impart God-honoring values and to build on your family's strengths. Best of all, you can be instrumental in instilling in your child that he is a person of value and worth. You will never regret the energy you invest in growing another human being.

Tom and Sherry Bushnell of the National Challenged Homeschoolers Associated Network (NATHHAN) acknowledge that the parents of special-needs kids are "trapped between a rock and a hard place. We are Christian families dealing with disability. We are concerned about a godly education for our children with special needs. For many of us, choosing to carefully educate our children with special needs at home is fun. Fun? Yes, we count the time invested in the lives of our special-needs children a well thought-out investment in the future. How many of us want to spend the rest of our lives with an ill-mannered, selfish, skill-less, unhappy, disabled adult? Not us! We may have been given a different role in life as a parent of a child with special needs, but we are not going to be miserable in our golden years."[2]

Look beyond the temporary frustration of raising a challenging child to see the person you will launch out of your home at adulthood. This is where your vision for homeschooling is birthed.

Will They Be OK?

Let's face it: Even parents who homeschool "normal" kids struggle with self-doubt. Include a disability or a difference in style or personality into the mix and the doubt can become crippling. How do we know we are doing the right thing for this child?

Regrettably, not much serious academic research has been done in this area. One encouraging study, however, set out to determine if ordinary parents, who were not certified teachers, could provide an adequate learning environment for special-needs kids. The sample was admittedly small—six elementary and two junior high students. The study looked at the amount of time students spent making academic responses. In this setting, that meant the amount of time spent responding to mom's teaching. Why is this significant? It is a truism of educational theory that increased academic engaged time (AET) will lead to an increase in achievement gains. The study showed that "generally, the measures of classroom ecology and achievement showed that home schools, when compared to special education programs, provided equal if not more advantageous instructional environments for children with learning disabilities."[3] Because of fewer children in the homeschool, they were afforded greater AET, so they gained more overall on standardized testing. The study's authors noted, "Ten times as much one-on-one instruction was observed in home school versus public school settings."[4] The testing showed homeschooled students made large gains in reading and written language while the public school students lost ground in reading and made only small gains in written language.[5]

The beauty of homeschooling is finally being recognized as a superior academic alternative. Homeschooling parents *know* they can accomplish more in a few hours of intense instruction than a classroom teacher with twenty or thirty students can accomplish in six hours of the school day. Now we know that this phenomenon has a name—academic engaged time. Because of the increased one-on-one time, homeschooling has been referred to as the Cadillac of education. Your challenging child should have as good of a ride!

Can I Do It?

I believe homeschooling is an extension of active, involved parenting. When our child is a challenging child, we must become more active and educated to learn to deal with their difficulties.

No matter how inept or inadequate we may feel, we must recognize that God uses us in our weakness. Moses complained, saying, "'O Lord, I have never been eloquent, neither in the past nor since you have spoken to your servant. I am slow of speech and tongue.' The LORD said to him,

'Who gave man his mouth? Who makes him deaf or mute? Who gives him sight or makes him blind? Is it not I, the LORD? Now go; I will help you speak and will teach you what to say'" (Exod. 4:10–12). Despite his hesitance and self-doubt, God used him mightily, just as God can use you in your child's life.

The Lord reminded Paul, "My grace is sufficient for you, for my power is made perfect in weakness" (2 Cor. 12:9). God will work through your weaknesses, in his grace, to accomplish what he wishes in your life and in your child's life.

I never believed I would encourage special-needs parents. The Lord put me in this place, and I am exceedingly blessed.

So where to begin? Like any spiritual journey, begin with prayer. Your goal is to facilitate your child's growth, but you will experience enormous growth as well. God may stretch you, but he is faithful.

There is an education of the mind
Which all require and parents only start
But there is training of a nobler kind
And that's the education of the heart
Lessons that are most difficult to give
Are faith and courage and the way to live.
                                            —Edgar Guest

CHAPTER TWO

Defining Terms

Disabilities, Differences, Discipline, Personality, and Learning Styles

Patience and perseverance have a magical effect before which difficulties disappear and obstacles vanish.

—John Quincy Adams

Carol's daughter, Kylie, is four years old. From birth to age two, she had recurrent, severe ear infections. Without a doubt, it was challenging.

Ages two to three brought some stability. Kylie, although full of energy, seemed more able to moderate her behavior and became easier for her mother to manage.

At age four the pendulum swung back the other way. Kylie became argumentative and disobedient. She would fight over the most minuscule request from her mother. Prepared to wage World War Three over her choice of shoes to wear on a cold day, Kylie was a force to be reckoned with!

Along with increased disagreeableness, Carol noticed Kylie had trouble staying on any task for very long. She would drift from activity to activity during playtime. When Carol tried to focus her on coloring, drawing, or any kind of table work, Kylie would attend for a few moments, then drift away to another activity. If Carol insisted that she sit still to complete a task, Kylie would brace for battle, and Carol would reluctantly allow her to go off to play. Carol was concerned because Kylie was approaching kindergarten age, and she worried she would not be able to teach Kylie the skills she needed.

Arthur, the oldest of three children, was fourteen. He had been homeschooled all his life. Although very bright and artistic, he was disorganized and forgetful. His mother was the opposite. She wanted the schoolwork done *her* way with *her* timing. Arthur usually got everything done, but he generally waited until the last minute to pull it off. While his work was hardly stellar or brilliant, it was correct and adequate. He and his mom continually butted heads due to his seeming lack of motivation. "He is doing OK, but he could be doing so much better," his mom reported.

Which of these families has a legitimate concern? One, the other, both, or neither?

A legitimate concern about your child's performance or behavior is *any* concern that is on your heart and mind. Sorting out whether it requires patience and maturity or professionals and medications is the tricky part.

I can recall many kids who were "different" in my own schooling. Rather than "learning disabled," they were simply referred to as "slow kids." A little extra attention and tutoring and they generally did OK. Still others were thought of as quiet and introverted (the loners) and were left to their own thoughts rather than being psychoanalyzed. Hyper kids were considered normal and energetic. Given sufficient outlets for their energy, they did just fine.

Today we are much quicker to assign a label or a disability. Our increasingly professionalized and compartmentalized society doesn't know what to do with a child who is different. While our country is noted for freedom of speech and freedom of expression, if your kid isn't like all the other kids on the block, you've got a problem! Regrettably, Christian homeschooling circles have been known to be particularly harsh and judgmental if a child is the least bit out of the ordinary.

The question for the parent remains: How do I sort out whether I have a real problem? Despite the impressive array of professionals and paraprofessionals available to help us, we are still the premier experts on our children. While we must not be in denial, we ultimately choose how we will deal with these precious creatures entrusted to our care.

Begin with prayer, knowledge, and observation. First, ask God to help you truly see what you are dealing with. Ask him for his wisdom—and then listen! Most healthy, well-balanced parents know in their heart when something is seriously wrong. Listen to that still voice of God as you set about unraveling your challenging child.

Along with your "inside work" with God, your next task is to educate yourself. Armed with the knowledge in this book and other materials referenced herein, you will be in a better position to pinpoint what, if any, action is required. There is no more helpless feeling than being uninformed and at the mercy of an array of professionals who have the potential to become involved in your child's life. With even a broad brush of knowledge you will be in a better position to make decisions on behalf of your child.

Finally, your own observations will be the most valuable part of this process. Chapter 9 presents some specific instructions for documenting behavior and responses, but ultimately you must look at your child through God's eyes. Sometimes we tired parents get caught in patterns of seeing and responding that keep us from seeing what is really happening. When you can separate yourself from your perhaps painful history with this child, you can see him through God's eyes. This perspective will give you wisdom and encouragement. God created this child for a purpose. It may take some digging and prayer to uncover it, but both you and your child will grow in the process.

Personality or Problem?

Have you heard that opposites attract? It is true that the positive and negative poles of a magnet will attract, but, alas, the human personality is more complex. Let's take a look at some examples.

In some families, it is not always the child who is laid back and the mother who is meticulous. One family I know has a structure-loving child and a mom who enjoys the ebb and flow of the day. This girl writes her own schedule and goals for the week so she knows what to expect. Mom would be happy to take a more relaxed approach, but the two have learned to blend their styles, and homeschooling is working splendidly for them.

In our home, one of my daughters must have a checklist of everything expected of her for the week. Any disruption to her plan is upsetting to her. On the other hand, while I rely heavily on schedules and plans, I am fluid in my approach to life because I never want to miss an opportunity to minister or to seize a chance to have an alternative learning experience. This can be quite upsetting for my daughter. When the interruptions occur and we are called away from our plan for the day, she laments, "When am I ever going to get all this work done?" I have learned to minimize disruptions affecting her as much as possible.

Be aware of personality differences you may have with your child and respect those differences. God made us unique so that we could complement and bless one another. Rather than constantly butting heads to accomplish the work part of homeschooling, there are ways to motivate and keep peace in the home.

Learning Styles

In another family, the mother was raised on a particular workbook curriculum. It worked well for her, and she reasoned it would work well for each of her six children. Within her brood, however, she has the entire spectrum of learning styles. She has two who respond beautifully and dutifully to workbooks—and four who do not! She has been so challenged and shaken by these four that she has considered sending them all off to school. Without the revelation and acceptance of learning style differences, she might miss the opportunity to have a lively, actively engaged homeschooling experience. Her challenge is to pull it all together to meet the learning styles of each child and keep Mom sane in the process. It can be done!

Discipline

Matt's parents divorced when he was six. Now nine, increasingly he is the terror of his Sunday school. His teacher dreads his entrance, although his attendance is inconsistent.

His mom is completely overwhelmed with the challenge of single parenting. She has chosen the path of least resistance and has given Matt freedom and choices far beyond what he can handle at his level of maturity. As a result, quite simply, Matt has become a brat! Well aware of his power, he continually pushes the boundaries with his mother, engaging in increasingly obnoxious behavior.

Mom can gain control by regaining her son's heart. It will take a major shift in her attitude and approach. It won't be easy, but I believe no child is beyond hope, and no parent should ever give up, no matter how discouraging the circumstances. By increasing her son's opportunity to have positive encounters and keeping the lines of communication open, this mother and son can reopen their hearts to one another and restore a proper, healthy relationship.

Differences

My son, Daniel, is an active little boy. Some have wondered if he is hyperactive, but he is a normal, active little boy. He can sit and do something academic, but he has to be in the right frame of mind. If his body is too busy and I am trying to engage his mind alone, we have a conflict.

On a good day, when I am tuned in to his needs, we do our phonics drill or our counting while he bounces on a mini-trampoline or runs around the big table in the dining room. Is he learning? Yes! And perhaps more effectively than if I made him sit still in a chair. In a traditional school, he would probably get a label. At home, he gets loved and accepted. Can he learn just as effectively whether standing up or while moving around? Absolutely.

There are also children who are strong in some areas and weak in others. Brent is an awesome violinist, but he struggles with math. His gifting is clearly in music, but he feels bad about himself because he is not good in everything. No one is good in everything! This child needs to be relieved from that unrealistic expectation so his strengths and talents can be celebrated! We all have weak areas, but they don't necessarily rise to the level of a disability. There is too much pressure to excel in every area of life, and it makes our children feel wholly inadequate.

We each have strengths and weaknesses, but we have calculators and spell checkers to help us cope. A difference might be a difficulty, but it does not rise to the level of a disability. A child who is a poor speller may have to work extra hard, but that does not mean she has a disability, absent other factors.

Disability

Another little girl, Molly, tries her best and makes little progress. She is a bright girl, but cannot remember letter sounds or the relationships of letters. She has been encouraged extensively, but she experiences interference with her memory storage and retrieval. She reverses her letters when she spells and cannot remember how to spell even the simplest words. This combination of average or above average intelligence and lowered achievement with some interference in the learning process—either due to visual, motor, auditory, or attention difficulties—is a classic disability. As muddy as that sounds, not all cases are that clear cut.

Carrie in Arizona has dealt with her son's confusing array of symptoms. He has had "speech problems that were persistent, emotional outbursts that were inappropriately timed, and a vast inability to sit still." It has taken her a great deal of time and energy to sort out her son's issues because his learning was being thwarted on a number of different levels.

According to the National Institute of Mental Health:

> LD [learning disability] is a disorder that affects people's ability to either interpret what they see and hear or to link information from different parts of the brain. These limitations can show up in many ways—as specific difficulties with spoken and written language, coordination, self-control, or attention. Such difficulties extend to schoolwork and can impede learning to read or write, or to do math. Learning disabilities can be life-long conditions that, in some cases, affect many parts of a person's life: school or work, daily routines, family life, and sometimes even friendships and play. In some people, many overlapping learning disabilities may be apparent. Other people may have a single, isolated learning problem that has little impact on other areas of their lives.[1]

A learning disability may not be readily apparent and may be difficult for families to process because the children *look* normal. In addition, many children show uneven learning patterns and demonstrate various challenges at different times in life. A clearer indication of a learning disability may be a struggle that exists over a long period of time. For example, a child who cannot distinguish certain words but outgrows this in six months would not be said to have a learning disability. (Each aspect of a learning disability will be fleshed out thoroughly in chapter 3.)

What Is the Law?

Why should a homeschooler be concerned with the law concerning learning disabilities when families have the constitutional right to home-school their children? I believe there are three sound reasons to be armed with this knowledge:

1. The more you know about your child's situation, the better position you will be in to make decisions about evaluations and therapies. Doing your research in this area allows you to explore *all* options. If your child had cancer, wouldn't you explore *all* avenues of treatment before dismissing any one of the alternatives?

2. Even if you choose not to avail yourself of public school services that are regulated by these laws, acquiring some knowledge and expertise in this area may enable you to minister to others who must make decisions about their child's treatment.

3. Alternatively, if you do decide to partner with the public school for services, now or in the future, you will want to be informed of the law and of your rights as the parent of a disabled child.

Three separate laws apply to children with learning disabilities. These laws are affectionately referred to as ADA, IDEA, and Section 504. Entire volumes have been written about these laws, and their meaning and applicability is still unfolding in case law. The following brief summary is intended to introduce the reader to the laws, not to give legal advice or to be a learned treatise on the subject.

The Americans with Disabilities Act of 1990 (ADA) is a set of broad civil rights legislation that requires reasonable measures to ensure that all public services and accommodations are available to people with disabilities, whether or not the providers of these services and accommodations receive any federal funding. The example of such an accommodation that leaps to mind is that of ramps to make a building wheelchair accessible.

Section 504 of the Rehabilitation Act of 1973 is also a civil rights law that requires reasonable accommodations to ensure that services are available, but applies specifically to programs or activities that receive federal funding. For either of these laws (ADA or Section 504), an individual with a disability is defined as one who (1) has a physical or mental impairment that substantially limits one or more life activities, (2) has a record of such an impairment, or (3) is regarded as having such an impairment. For purposes of these laws, any hindrance to the process of learning would be considered an impairment that significantly limits life activities.

These two laws say that people with disabilities must be accommodated, but there is no mention of how this accommodation is to be funded. Thus, we have the next law, the Individuals with Disabilities Education Act (IDEA), amended in 1997. IDEA is the federal vehicle that provides funding to education agencies to guarantee services to children with disabilities. It is narrower in scope and covers fewer children.

IDEA guarantees that children who qualify in one of thirteen categories will be given a free and appropriate education (FAPE) in the least restrictive environment (LRE) possible. The categories are autism, deaf-blindness, deafness, emotional disturbance, hearing impairment, mental retardation, multiple disabilities, orthopedic impairment, other health impairment, specific learning disability, speech or language impairment, traumatic brain injury, and visual impairment including blindness. When the suggestion of one of these issues is brought to the attention of the school, an individualized evaluation is required, which is reviewed yearly. A re-evaluation is required every three years. If a child is deemed to be disabled, an individualized educational program (IEP) is prepared, which gives specific actions to be taken on behalf of the child.

The IDEA also serves infants and toddlers with disabilities who need intervention services. A child who is experiencing developmental delays in one of the following areas is eligible for services: cognitive development, physical development (including vision and hearing), communication development, social or emotional development, adaptive development or delay. Thus, if you are the parent of a child not yet of school age, programs and services are available through the government to assist you. For infants and toddlers aged birth through two, services are provided through an *early intervention* system that may be run by the Health Department in the state, or another department such as the Department of Education. If you are a parent and you would like to find out more about early intervention in your state and how to have your child evaluated at no cost to you, ask your child's pediatrician to put you in touch with the early intervention system in your community or region, or contact the pediatrics department in a local hospital and ask who to call to find out about early intervention services in your area.

All children who are covered by IDEA also are covered by Section 504, but not all 504 children are covered by IDEA because Section 504 provides a broader definition—the three-pronged test mentioned above—of a disability. A child who does not possess one of the thirteen listed disabilities under IDEA may still receive special services under Section 504. However, parents should be aware that if their child only qualifies for special services under Section 504, no federal funds are provided for this type of child, and the school must fund any additional assistance from its own budget.

What are the additional conditions that are covered under Section 504? Under this regulation a physical or mental impairment is defined as any physiological disorder or condition, cosmetic disfigurement, or anatomical loss affecting one or more of the following body systems: neurological, musculoskeletal, special sense organs, respiratory including speech organs, cardiovascular, reproductive, digestive, genito-urinary, hemic and lymphatic, skin or endocrine; or any mental or psychological disorder, such as mental retardation, organic brain syndrome, emotional or mental illness, and specific learning disabilities.

The impairment must have a substantial limitation on one or more major life activities. It is suggested that both academic and nonacademic activities need to be considered. Some examples are students with communicable diseases (like hepatitis), students with temporary disabilities arising from accidents, students with allergies or asthma, students with environmental illnesses, and students who are drug-addicted or alcoholic, as long as they are not currently using illegal drugs. In addition, children who have ADHD without a concurrent learning disability frequently fall into the Section 504 category.

Remember that homeschooling families need not be concerned about the law unless they choose to avail themselves of public services in the public school system. These laws serve as a sifting-out process to determine who will receive the free services of the schools. With limited resources and personnel, they are the legislature's mechanism to see that funds are placed where they are most warranted.

In the homeschool, we place our time and treasure where our heart is—with our children. If there is one sheep lagging behind, we lovingly gather it up and bring it along—no stigma, no funding problems, no sifting out process. All our children are worthy in God's eyes.

In chapter 9 we will discuss evaluations, including how to obtain one from your local public school. In the next chapter, we'll discuss the characteristics of specific disabilities.

CHAPTER THREE

A Disability Primer

Trouble is only opportunity in work clothes.
—Henry Kaiser

An informal park play date several years ago opened my eyes to how often learning issues occur. Marilyn shared that her daughter had been evaluated by the reading specialist at school because she was slow to learn her letter sounds. Another mother of a sixteen-year-old lamented the vast sums of money they were spending to send their teen to a private tutoring chain, but it was the only thing they had found that helped him raise his grades. Sheila laughed and said she wished she could afford to send her daughter to a tutor because their nightly sessions over arithmetic were long and often heated. In this one group of five women hanging out at the local park, four of us had academic struggles with our children.

According to the United States Department of Education, as many as one out of five Americans have a learning disability. Almost three million children have some form of learning disability and receive special education in school.[1] It is reasonable to assume that the same percentage applies to the homeschool population.

Knowledge is powerful, yet there are advantages and disadvantages to obtaining a diagnosis of your child. Such a diagnosis may resolve years of questioning and doubt about your child and your parenting ability. It may be a relief to discover that something you thought was a character defect is truly beyond the child's control. Armed with this knowledge, you can research strategies and solutions for working with and teaching your child. Otherwise, you are driving blindfolded down a dark alley. A diagnosis is also something that the various professionals you may encounter will understand. Your ADHD child, coupled with overtones of ODD (Oppositional Defiant Disorder), will be immediately recognized by professionals and fellow suffering parents.

Of course, this same information also may be a liability. Your child may feel differently when she knows she is PDD (Pervasive Developmental Disorder) or e-i-e-i-o (think of "Old MacDonald's Farm") and may perceive herself as damaged goods. The label may last through her entire schooling, contributing to low self-esteem. Conversely, your child may experience the freeing relief that a diagnosis can bring. Understanding why she struggles can make her more determined to overcome or lessen those struggles.

In an ideal world, everyone would readily accept the differences in children and others. Parents, however, can provide that acceptance—at least within the home. Homeschooling can be liberating for a slower learner, and you will have the joy of witnessing when the child eventually does blossom.

A *learning disability* is present when a child has normal or above normal intelligence, but is underachieving in one or more academic areas despite efforts to learn. There is a significant discrepancy between the child's intelligence and achievement. The academic areas delineated by federal law are:

- basic reading skills
- reading comprehension

- written expression (including spelling)
- listening comprehension
- oral expression
- mathematics calculations and mathematics reasoning

How We Learn

The learning process can be broken down into a few simple steps.

PERCEPTION

Information is received through the sensory systems: the eyes (visual), the ears (auditory), the fingers and hands (kinesthetic), the nose (smell), and the mouth (taste). This is the input stage. The auditory and visual systems are most often used in traditional schools, with some hands-on activities.

A child who has trouble with visual input might be said to have a visual perception disability. A visual perception issue might involve letter reversal or rotation, visual figure-ground difficulty, or trouble judging distances. This is the child who reads w-a-s for s-a-w, who becomes completely overwhelmed when confronted with a busy workbook page of math problems, and who judges distances so poorly that a game of catch presents significant challenges to the child's visual/motor systems.

The child who struggles with an auditory deficiency might be said to have an auditory perception disability. Auditory perception disability can manifest itself as difficulty distinguishing subtle differences in sound, auditory figure-ground problems, or an auditory lag—processing information at a slightly slower rate than most children.

Imagine this child in a noisy classroom. The teacher is talking, but the child cannot focus on her because there are other sounds competing for his attention—the buzz of the air conditioner, the sounds of children walking in the hall, and the ticking of the clock. The teacher calls out the word *dish* to spell as a test word, but the child hears the word as *fish*. After he hears the word, he must repeat it to himself several times in order to retain it in his memory.

Some children may have trouble with both types of perception, such as seeing what is written on a blackboard and understanding verbal explanations. Put this child in a noisy room with lots of colorful posters on the walls and he will go into sensory overload! Yet this is precisely the atmosphere in many cheerful, busy classrooms across America. While it might be stimulating and fun for the average child, for the child with visual or auditory disabilities, such an environment is torture.

INTEGRATION

Once information works its way through neural pathways to the brain, it must be integrated or understood. A child may experience difficulty with integration as evidenced by:
- having trouble sequencing the information, such as remembering the beginning, middle, and end of a story;
- keeping the correct sequence of math problems;
- remembering the days of the week and the months of the year; or
- remembering the correct sequence of words to spell them correctly, such as remembering the difference between s-a-w and w-a-s.

Another way integration difficulty manifests itself is by having difficulty with organization. The child may have trouble organizing his thoughts or his room. This child also may listen carefully to multistep directions but then forget what she is supposed to do on the way to do it! For example, when I tell my daughter to go upstairs, put on her socks, and turn off the light, she may head for her bedroom, then forget why she was sent there.

RETENTION

The next step in learning is to process the information in some fashion so it can be stored into memory. In order to be stored, it must be categorized and classified or pegged onto information that is already known. For example, when a child has learned to add, subtraction can be presented as the inverse of addition. This allows the child to peg new information (subtraction) onto something with which he is already familiar (addition).

Another aspect of processing information is remembering information. Memory may be short-term or long-term. A child with difficulties may have excellent recall in one, the other, or neither. Memory can be increased by increasing the number of senses involved in the reception of the information. For example, when teaching math concepts, the use of manipulatives is essential for these children because it involves both the visual and tactile learning avenues. Using a number line to jump backward for subtraction would add a further learning dimension.

A child with retention problems also requires significantly greater repetitions for retention to occur. An average child might take twenty-two exposures to a piece of information to learn and retain it. For the child with a learning disability, it will take many more exposures than that, or require additional techniques to solidify the information.

RETRIEVAL

Lastly, information must be retrieved for later use. In a traditional school setting, high value is placed on remembering and repeating information. Any inability to retrieve information quickly can be disastrous for school functioning.

Often learning disabled children require more time to retrieve information. Joan Harwell, in her book *The Complete Learning Disabilities Handbook,* writes, "It is worthwhile to note that when individuals with LD are given unlimited time to show what they know, they can sometimes match the performance of their nondisabled peers."[2] For this very reason, a common accommodation for a learning disabled child is untimed testing. It affords them the opportunity to truly display what they know, unhindered by how fast they can access it.

EXPRESSION

The final process of learning is the expression of information, or its output. In the traditional school, this is speaking and writing. A child who cannot organize his thoughts to speak coherently or who cannot compose his thoughts to express himself in writing will suffer greatly in the classroom. Introduce any number and types of interferences, and it denigrates the overall learning process.

◆ ◆ ◆

When a child experiences difficulty in learning, there is usually some interference in one or more of the above processes. It is more than learning style—a preference in the way one takes in information. It is more than a weakness in one area, such as one who is simply weak in math or spelling. A child with a learning disability has a nervous system that has been wired differently.

Think about the steps in reading. The child sees the word *cat*. The brain recognizes the phonemes: c-a-t. He links the sounds and identifies the word. Finally, the brain applies meaning to the word using stored vocabulary, reasoning, intelligence, and experience. Given the potential for disruption at any stage in this process, it can be seen how complex it is to learn to read.

Imagine you just purchased a new refrigerator. Every time you open the door, the inside light turns off. When you turn the thermostat down, the temperature inside the refrigerator goes up. The doors inside are attached upside down, and the shelves are hung sideways so that anything placed on them slides to the floor of the unit. You become angry with the refrigerator for not responding the way you expected it to or the way you have seen refrigerators respond in the past. This is how it feels to the child with a learning disability when he is forced to perform in ways his brain is not wired to handle.

If the "wiring" is in the area of the brain having to do with language, the child may have a language disability, either receptive or expressive. If the area of the brain in question has to do with the use of the muscles, it may manifest as a motor disability. If the large muscles are involved, it affects gross motor skills. If small muscles are involved, it affects fine motor skills. If the wiring of the brain is misfiring in the area that allows concentration and filters out distractions, the child might be hyperactive or distractible.

Before my daughter was diagnosed, I viewed her behavior and reactions as disobedience. She was, I thought, just a stubborn, strong-willed child, and it was my job to bring her into submission. While she may have some stubborn, strong-willed tendencies, I am so grateful to know that her brain is wired like that refrigerator mentioned on the previous page. There is no need for me to be angry with her or to compare her to other children. My job is to teach her how to learn within the context of her unique set of strengths and weaknesses.

Watch Out! Early Warning Signs of Learning Problems

Unless a child has been referred to an early intervention program (see chap. 2), a learning disability may not be recognized until the child is of school age. Due to budget and personnel restraints, many schools take a wait-and-see attitude about the struggling child and may not recognize or offer assistance until the child is functioning at least two years behind grade level. Legally, public schools may not refuse services, but they may impose conditions on eligibility, such as the child being sufficiently behind academically, to warrant assistance with special services.

I believe we in the homeschooling community must be particularly vigilant. While we do not want to rush our children into formal academics, we must not mistake a "late bloomer" for a child with real learning needs. The reality is that the longer a true problem remains unrecognized and the parents wait to get help, the more likely the student's problems will linger or even worsen. Learning disabilities do not go away simply with wishing, hoping, praying, or waiting. They require intervention, and an educated, knowledgeable parent can provide that intervention.

The early warning signs to monitor are:

1. *Developmental delays.* Children achieve developmental milestones at different rates and times. Remember, a delay does not necessarily

indicate a disability, because children have their own timetables. Nonetheless, here are some general markers to watch for:

- 3 to 6 months: follows movement with eyes, rolls from side to side, holds head upright, begins to reach for a desired object, rolls over
- 9 months: gets up on hands and knees, sits without support, tracks an object, feeds self with hands, stands with support
- 12 months: crawls, looks at pictures, makes marks on a paper, waves good-bye, plays pat-a-cake, pulls self up
- 18 months: walks, stacks blocks, recognizes shapes, says a few words, can remove simple garments
- 24 months: pretends, likes nursery rhymes, can point to pictures, jumps in place, runs, can make two- to three-word sentences
- 36 months: sorts objects, walks up and down stairs, sings, can use scissors, can speak understandably, uses the toilet with help, draws simple pictures, feeds and dresses self
- 48 months: tells a simple story, climbs a slide, catches and kicks a ball, colors reasonably within the lines, classifies pictures, copies shapes, laces shoes, hops on one foot, counts to five, names some colors, talks in sentences, shares and plays with others
- 60 months: can cut and paste, copies a pattern of beads, taps and claps a rhythm, plays a simple game, prints a few letters, follows directions, counts up to four objects, rote counts to ten, skips, catches a ball, buttons and ties shoes, can repeat a nursery rhyme, draws a person that includes most features, compares differences between pictures

2. *Inconsistent performance.* I always was amazed at the inconsistency of my own daughter. On a good day she could read like a champion. On a bad day she could not remember how to read the word *the.* I have since learned that this is typical of the uneven brain development in these children. Some are whizzes in math, but they cannot compose a sentence. If you see this inconsistency in your child, don't be too quick to blame it on lack of discipline. Your child's brain may indeed be the cause of the inconsistency.

3. *Loss of interest in learning.* There is no greater parental joy than to watch a child's enthusiasm. Life with an inquisitive child is peppered with questions, such as, "Why do butterflies have to die?" or "Are there dogs in heaven?" If you have started formal "teaching" with your child and this enthusiasm has waned, it may be because learning has become too difficult for her and thus something to be avoided.

4. *Unexpected underachievement.* Dips and peaks in a child's school performance are to be expected. Some children are just a bit slower learning to read, write, or do math. Parents should pay particularly close attention when the difficulty and complexity of schooling ramps up. As grade levels progress, increasingly difficult assignments are required and larger amounts of information are presented. This may cause your child to stumble. If he does not bounce back within that academic year, it may be more than a temporary dip.

5. *Persistent behavioral or emotional problems.* When a child has problems with perception (hearing, remembering, seeing), it can manifest as rudeness or defiance. The stress from overloading an already taxed brain can lead to acting out behavior. Consider this: the brain functions much like a computer. Data comes in via a keyboard, disk, or CD. It outputs data through printing, viewing on the screen, or copying to a file. Sometimes a computer will "lock up" or significantly slow down when overloaded with too many inputs. The software may have miscoded lines that cause it to go in "do loops" or repetitive cycles until broken. If certain pathways are not properly imprinted on the computer's microchip, synapses will malfunction and cause glitches in computation and decoding. The computer has enough sense to shut down when overloaded. People, however, do not. Our daughter would have mercurial changes in mood. We blamed it on a deficit of character. In reality, it was from having a brain so taxed that she felt her head might explode!

6. *Declining confidence and self-esteem.* These are the most common "side effects" of a learning problem. Children feel bad about themselves. They don't feel normal or accepted by others. Repeated frustration and failure can cause confidence and self-esteem to plummet. An inept teacher

may inadvertently ridicule a child through verbal admonitions or unintentional nonverbal body cues.

◆ ◆ ◆

Highlighting these early warning signs is intended to inform, not frighten, you. Do you see your child in any of these descriptions? Parents, you know your child better than anyone else. What does your gut tell you?

Attention Deficit Disorder

I thought I knew and understood Attention-Deficit/Hyperactivity Disorder (ADHD). It was the child who bounced off the walls and couldn't concentrate for more than two seconds, right?

Yes and no. There are a number of spectrums of ADHD. One is Attention-Deficit/Hyperactivity Disorder (ADHD). The other is Undifferentiated Attention-Deficit Disorder (without hyperactivity), which denotes a more depressive, inattentive aspect. The child's mind may drift or jump abruptly from thought to thought. Fiona in Virginia shared, "I knew one of my daughters was a 'space case.' That led me to a doctor who diagnosed her with ADD-inattentive type." The third type of ADD is a combination of these two, or a combined diagnosis.

I need to stress here that ADHD is *not* a learning disability, and a learning disability does not necessarily include ADHD. A learning disability, as we have been discussing it herein, is a language-based disorder affecting reading. ADHD is an overriding inability to focus or sustain attention. It is common, however, for ADHD students also to have learning disabilities.

If a child is not paying attention, for whatever reason, he can't learn. Attention is critical for the other systems of learning to engage. In other words, a child can have good visual, auditory, and motor processing, but not be attending because of attention issues. Conversely, attention issues *plus* an interference with one of the other systems can potentially be a challenging mountain for the child to climb.

In the early 1990s the U.S. Department of Education finally recognized ADHD as an official disability. Children now may receive special services in the public schools if the disorder affects their educational performance.

The characteristics of all such challenges are spelled out in the American Psychiatric Association's *Diagnostic and Statistical Manual of Mental Disorders* (DSM-IV).[3] Let's look at the ADHD characteristics of the inattentive type, the hyperactive/impulsive type, and combined type.

1. ATTENTION-DEFICIT/HYPERACTIVITY DISORDER, PREDOMINANTLY INATTENTIVE TYPE

The student must have exhibited six or more of the following symptoms of inattention for at least six months:

- often fails to give close attention to details or makes careless mistakes in schoolwork, work, or other activities
- often has difficulty sustaining attention to tasks or play activities
- often does not seem to listen when spoken to directly
- often does not follow through on instructions and fails to finish schoolwork, chores, or duties in the workplace (not due to oppositional behavior or failure to understand instructions)
- often has difficulty organizing tasks and activities
- often avoids, dislikes, or is reluctant to engage in tasks that require sustained mental effort (such as schoolwork or homework)
- often loses things necessary for tasks or activities (e.g., toys, school assignments, pencils, books, or tools)
- is often easily distracted by extraneous stimuli
- is often forgetful in daily activities

An estimated 30 percent of all children who have ADHD suffer from this set of symptoms.

2. ATTENTION-DEFICIT/HYPERACTIVITY DISORDER, PREDOMINANTLY HYPERACTIVE-IMPULSIVE TYPE

This diagnosis is applicable if the student has six or more symptoms of hyperactivity-impulsivity that have persisted for at least six months:

Hyperactivity
- often fidgets with hands or feet or squirms in seat
- often leaves seat in classroom or in other situations when remaining seated is expected
- often runs about or climbs excessively in situations in which it is inappropriate (in adolescents or adults, may be limited to subjective feelings of restlessness)
- often has difficulty playing or engaging in leisure activities quietly
- is often "on the go" or acts as if "driven by a motor"
- often talks excessively

Impulsivity
- often blurts out answers before questions have been completed
- often has difficulty awaiting their turn
- often interrupts or intrudes on others (e.g., butts into conversations or games)

Of all children diagnosed with ADHD, 10 percent exhibit this constellation of symptoms.

3. ATTENTION-DEFICIT/HYPERACTIVITY DISORDER, COMBINED TYPE

This type requires the presence of six or more symptoms of inattention and six or more symptoms of hyperactivity-impulsivity that have persisted for at least six months. This category represents 60 percent of children who are diagnosed with ADHD.

According to the authors of *The Parents' Complete Special Education Guide,* the peak age for referral of children suspected of having ADHD is between eight and ten.[4] As stated in each category, symptoms must have been of at least six months duration and not due to some other disorder. Most children exhibit some of these symptoms at one point or another. It is duration and severity that create a concern.

Visual Perception Disability

A visual perception disability indicates that the child has trouble making sense of what they see. It is not a problem with eyesight but with how the brain perceives visual input. The problem is in understanding a visual image. The child may not recognize, organize, interpret, or remember what he sees. The letters most often confused are d, b, p, and q—essentially the same figure placed in different positions in space. Many young children have trouble making these distinctions, but when the difficulty extends beyond the age of five or six, it may indicate a problem. Since a great deal of what goes on in school involves making visual distinctions, this places the child at a pronounced disadvantage.

Sometimes a visual problem manifests itself as a figure/ground issue. The child will look at a large page of math problems and feel completely overwhelmed visually because she cannot visually sort out one problem from the other. She has difficulty focusing on one area when there are other visual inputs in the background. These children may skip words or lines when reading or read the same line twice. There are many ways to help this child, such as cutting the problem page into pieces or creating a little viewing box so that only one problem is seen at a time.

A visual difficulty also may involve difficulty judging distances, such as a depth perception issue. A child's carelessness may actually be because he has difficulty perceiving distances and spacial relationships. This child may fall off his seat or knock things over because of visual misjudgment.

Think about all the perceptual processes involved in the simple act of catching a ball. It involves the visual (focusing on the ball), depth perception (to judge the position and path of the ball), and the motor system (to figure out where and when to move). This seemingly simple task can be enormously complicated for a child with visual processing issues.

The following list of observable behavioral patterns[5] may indicate a visual perception issue:

Visual Perception Disability Checklist
Writing
- dislikes and avoids writing
- delay in learning to write
- papers are messy and incomplete with many cross-outs and erasures

- difficulty remembering shapes of letters and numbers
- frequent letter and number reversals
- uneven spacing between letters and words
- omits letters from words and words from sentences
- inaccurate copying
- poor spelling (spells phonetically)
- cannot spot errors in own work
- difficulty preparing outlines and organizing written work

Reading

- confuses similar-looking letters (b and d, p and q)
- difficulty recognizing and remembering "sight" words (but can sometimes sound words out phonetically)
- frequently loses place when reading
- confuses similar-looking words (*bread* and *beard*)
- reverses words (reads *was* for *saw*)
- has trouble finding letters in words or words in sentences
- poor memory for printed words (also number sequences, diagrams, illustrations, and so on)
- poor comprehension of main ideas and themes

Math

- poor alignment of problems, resulting in computation errors
- difficulty memorizing math facts, multiplication tables, formulas, and equations
- trouble interpreting graphs, charts, and diagrams
- difficulty with higher-level math concepts

Related problems

- confuses right and left
- difficulty estimating time, being on time
- poor sense of direction; slow to learn his or her way around a new place
- difficulty judging speed and distance (interferes with many games; can be a problem when driving a car)
- has trouble "getting to the point"; becomes bogged down in details

- does not pick up on other peoples' moods and feelings (results in often saying the wrong thing at the wrong time)
- poor planning and organizational skills
- often loses things; cannot spot objects "in plain sight"
- distaste for puzzles, mazes, or other activities with a strong visual element
- difficulty perceiving strategies for being successful in games (may not understand the goal)

Language/Auditory Processing Disability

This child has trouble with discrimination of subtle differences in sound and may have a difficult time with phonics because he or she cannot hear the difference between sounds—for example, *buh* and *duh*. The English language is made up of units of sound called *phonemes*. Not only does each letter represent a sound, but letters also are combined to produce sounds. The incredible variety of possibilities leaves lots of room for error for the child with an auditory processing disorder.

This child also may have auditory figure/ground problems. If there is more than one sound present, they do not know what to attend to. Since there is rarely only one auditory stimulus going on at a time, what we may interpret as inattention or disobedience may be the child's literal inability to attend to one stimulus in the midst of many. A beginning strategy here is to establish eye contact with the child before speaking to her.

This child may have a hard time with the sequence of language or remembering a series of verbal commands. She may process verbal information slowly and be slow to get jokes or to comprehend subtle nuances of language. Sometimes she simply experiences difficulty in trying to keep up with the speed of language, resulting in an auditory lag. My own son often whispers to himself something I have spoken before he can fully process it.

The following checklist[6] presents things to look for in assessing a language/auditory processing disability.

Language/Auditory Processing Disability Checklist

Speech and language comprehension

- delay in learning to speak
- does not modulate tone of voice appropriately; speaks in monotone, or too loud
- has problems naming objects or people
- uses vague, imprecise language; has a small vocabulary
- speech is slow or halting; uses verbal "stalling" mechanisms ("uh," "um," "you know")
- uses poor grammar
- frequently mispronounces words
- confuses words with similar sounds (such as *frustrate* and *fluctuate*; may produce hybrid words, such as *flustrate*)
- often uses hand gestures and body language to help convey message
- avoids talking (especially in front of strangers, authority figures, or groups)
- insensitive to rhymes
- little interest in books or stories
- does not respond appropriately to questions (replies, "Monday" when asked, "Where do you go to school?")
- frequently does not understand or remember instructions

Reading

- significant delay in learning to read
- difficulty naming letters
- problems associating letters with sounds, discriminating between sounds in words, and blending sounds into words
- difficulty analyzing sound sequences; frequent sequencing errors (such as reading *snug* for *sung*)
- guesses at unfamiliar words rather than applying word analysis skills
- reads very slowly; oral reading deteriorates within a few sentences (due to declining ability to retrieve sounds rapidly from memory)

- comprehension for what has been read is consistently poor or deteriorates when sentences become longer and more complex
- poor retention of new vocabulary words
- dislikes and avoids reading

Writing

- written assignments are short or incomplete; often characterized by brief sentences and limited vocabulary
- problems with grammar persist
- bizarre spelling errors (not phonetic); student may be unable to decipher own spelling
- ideas in written assignments are poorly organized and not logically presented
- little theme development; students are more likely to write lists of points or events than provide details or develop ideas, characters, or plot
- on tests, consistently does better with multiple-choice questions than essays or filling in blanks

Math

- slow response during math-fact drills due to problems with number retrieval
- difficulty with word problems due to poor language comprehension
- problems with higher-level math due to difficulties with analysis and logical reasoning

Related problems

- "garbles" telephone messages; misunderstands what is heard on radio or TV
- difficulty with verbal reasoning; may understand all the words in the proverb "A rolling stone gathers no moss" but be unable to explain what it means; may find it hard to draw logical conclusions
- problems understanding puns and jokes; may not detect teasing
- difficulty making comparisons and classifying objects or ideas
- difficulty remembering information or producing facts or ideas on demand

- difficulty presenting a story or directions in logical order
- types of problems encountered during learning English are likely to be repeated when studying a foreign language
- difficulty joining or maintaining conversations

Motor/Sensory Integration Disability

These children cannot fully control their small muscles. They may be functioning at normal intellectual capacity, but their written communication skills are impaired.

Writing, drawing, copying, and taking notes are all extremely difficult for this child. He or she may spill things and make mistakes during hands-on activities. Unlike other disorders, this tends to be a more obvious disability. Other children may be quicker to notice the child's difficulty, unlike the child who has trouble with other types of processing.

It is interesting to note that large motor skills may remain relatively unaffected, and these children can even be excellent athletes!

Fine Motor Disability Checklist[7]
At home
- appears awkward and clumsy; often drops, spills, or knocks things over
- has difficulty picking up and using small objects, such as puzzle pieces or Legos
- has trouble with buttons, hooks, and zippers when dressing; finds it very difficult to tie shoes
- unsuccessful in games and activities that involve hand skills (cat's cradle, piano lessons, basketball)
- poor coloring ability; cannot keep within lines
- artwork looks immature for age (drawings from imagination are usually better than efforts at copying designs)
- difficulty using scissors
- awkward pencil grip (may hold pencil too loosely or too tightly)
- delay in learning to write; writing is large and immature; letters and numbers are poorly formed

- may be delayed in learning to speak or have articulation problems

At school

- poor handwriting (sloppy, illegible, poor spacing, inconsistent letter size, no consistent style, strays from lines on paper)
- papers are messy (torn and crumpled with many cross-outs, smudges, and incomplete erasures)
- marked slowness, exceptional effort, and frustration noted during writing tasks
- dislike and avoidance of writing or drawing
- written efforts are short and often incomplete
- content/style of written assignments is poor (primary focus is on achieving legibility)
- in severe cases, difficulty learning keyboarding skills

Dyslexia vs. Language-Learning Disability

The term *dyslexia* is often used to describe the broad spectrum of reading disorders, but it actually has a specific, narrow meaning. Dr. Sally Shaywitz, author of *Overcoming Dyslexia,* explains the distinction this way: "In *developmental dyslexia* the phonologic weakness is primary, other components of the language system are intact, and the reading impairment is at the level of decoding the single word, initially accurately and later fluently. . . . In *language-learning disability* the primary deficit involves all aspects of language, including both the sounds and the meanings of words. The reading difficulty is at the level of both decoding and comprehension."[8] The suggestions and solutions of special educators, many of which are contained in this book, for dealing with reading issues apply to both types of disability.

Dyscalculia *is defined as a disturbance
in the ability to calculate.*
Dysgraphia *is a disturbance in the
ability to write.
For a complete treatment of dyslexia,*

see Overcoming Dyslexia *by Sally
Shaywitz, M.D. (New York: Alfred A.
Knopf, 2003).*

Take Your Child's Learning "Pulse"

When a child is ill, we take his or her temperature and observe the vital signs. We need to do the same with our child's learning. If your challenge with your child is in the area of a learning disability, take your child's academic pulse once or twice a year. If they are writing, have them do the following assignment for you. Keep it as a standard against which to benchmark their progress.

1. Have him write his name and the date.
2. Have him draw a person.
3. Have him write the alphabet.
4. Give him ten words to spell (use ones that you are pretty sure he can spell well).
5. Have him write three to five sentences that you dictate (choose ones at his reading level).
6. Have him write three to five sentences about a topic of his choosing.
7. Copy some grade-level math problems and let him work them independently.
8. Have him read a passage from a book into a tape recorder.

Save these items in a progress folder. Once or twice a year repeat the assignment and check your child's progress.

You Are Not Alone

When we first received our daughter's diagnosis, we were certain that no one else in the world had our problems, even though we knew that to be untrue. We operated under the cloud of terminal uniqueness and feared we would never find anyone to understand or help us with our issues.

The following information is from www.SchwabLearning.org, a tremendous resource for information and encouragement when dealing with learning disabilities:

- 2.9 million students are currently receiving special education services for learning disabilities in the United States (source: Twenty-Third Annual Report to Congress, 2001).

- 51 percent of students receiving special education services through the public schools are identified as having learning disabilities (source: Twenty-Third Annual Report to Congress, 2001).

- The majority of individuals with learning disabilities have difficulty in the area of reading (source: President's Commission on Excellence in Special Education, 2002).

- 44 percent of parents who noticed their child exhibiting signs of difficulty with learning waited a year or more before acknowledging their child might have a serious problem (source: Roper Starch Poll: Measuring Progress in Public and Parental Understanding of Learning Disabilities).

- 27 percent of children with learning disabilities drop out of high school (source: Twenty-Third Annual Report to Congress, 2001).

- 40 percent of full-time college freshmen with disabilities attending four-year colleges reported having a learning disability (source: Health Resource Center, 2001).

- In the past nine years, the percentage of students who spend 80 percent or more of their time in school in special education classes increased from 21 to 45 percent (source: Twenty-Third Annual Report to Congress, 2001).

- 29 percent of undergraduate students with disabilities reported having a learning disability (source: National Center for Education Statistics, 2000).

- Only 13 percent of students with learning disabilities (compared to 53 percent of students in the general population) have attended a four-year post-secondary school program within two years of leaving high school (source: National Longitudinal Transition Study, 1994).

• 46 percent of all students with disabilities enrolled at two-year and four-year post-secondary education institutions reported having learning disabilities (source: National Center for Education Statistics, 2000).

Do not be anxious about anything, but in everything, by prayer and petition, with thanksgiving, present your requests to God. And the peace of God, which transcends all understanding, will guard your hearts and your minds in Christ Jesus.

—Philippians 4:6–7

CHAPTER FOUR

Attention Disorders

Teaching the Distractible Child

I have learned that success is to be measured not so much by the position one has reached in life as by the obstacles he has overcome while trying to succeed.

—Booker T. Washington

The same daughter who could not concentrate because the snow was bothering her also has a habit of becoming obsessed with scratching her leg when confronted with a challenge. She becomes so focused on a real or imagined itch that she cannot attend to her work. She sometimes scratches and cries in frustration, frequently falling off her chair in the process.

This is an example of the inattentive aspect of ADHD. At the other end of the spectrum is the child who seems constitutionally unable to remain still long enough to attend. He literally and figuratively bounces off the walls with unbridled energy and cannot focus on the task at hand.

Carol Barnier captured the essence of such a challenge of teaching a distractible child when she recounted this story of her son. She asked him why he had been spitting on a hot light bulb. "Because I liked the sizzle" was his response.[1] Teaching a distractible child is teaching a child who seeks the sizzle in everything. How are you going to channel that for the more active child? For the inattentive child, how are you going to wake up the brain to engage it productively?

Many in society view such children as undisciplined "brats." As parents, the challenge is to sort out: Is he a brat, or is there a problem? The real test seems to be:

- If you are consistent in routines and discipline,
- if your child knows what to expect,
- if you apply consequences regularly and fairly, and
- if the inattentive or out-of-control behavior continues, you may have a problem.

Before you conclude that the child is the problem, try to modify the environment and modify your approach. When all of those efforts fail, then it might be time to look at attention disorders.

In addition, you must determine if your child is just a different kind of learner. ADHD kids are usually very kinesthetic and tactile and are in anguish when they have to sit in a neat row like all the other students and do page after page of math problems. If your child is in the traditional school setting, you must question: Is the problem with the student or with the system?

In the homeschool setting, many of these issues are resolved. Instead of the hustle and bustle of the classroom, the parent can create a quieter atmosphere. Class size is definitely smaller! In the home the child can be free to explore learning strategies that use their strengths instead of just focusing on their weaknesses.

In many ways, ADHD is a hidden challenge. The child has no apparent physical defect and acts normal some of the time. Others may dismiss your concerns with the observation that "She looks normal. What could be wrong with her?" Under the laws protecting those with disabilities, ADHD *can* be considered a disability. When we learn how to channel the energy and creativity while giving support and an appropriate learning environment, these children can blossom!

Why Are There So Many ADHD Children?

It seems we all know someone whose kid is ADHD. Are there really more kids with this "disorder," or are we rearing children differently? Does more public knowledge about this problem lead to more diagnoses? Or are teachers and educators using it as a crutch to deal with children who do not respond to traditional methods of teaching and parenting?

If life doesn't happen in ten-second sound bites with a thirty-minute resolution of the problem, kids tune out. This is what they have come to expect in our media-rich environment. The pace of life is so fast and the barrage of messages so intense that attention spans are affected. Previous generations could listen to a three-hour sermon. Today, if our attention isn't captured in the first fifteen seconds, forget it! Even if you can catch attention, the average attention span for an adult is six minutes.

In his thought-provoking book *The Myth of the A.D.D. Child,* Thomas Armstrong, Ph.D., reports, "Today's child is a scanner. His experience with electronic media has taught him to scan life the way his eye scans a television set or his ears scan auditory signals from a radio or stereo speaker. Many of these fast-paced, media-fed kids may be labeled A.D.D. by adults who live life in the slow lane. What is considered a disease or disorder by parents or professionals may in fact be, for some kids at least, an entirely healthy response to a faster cultural tempo."[2]

Children aren't given a chance to practice paying attention. Remember playing board games, or cards, or even yard games? You had to learn to wait your turn and pay attention while waiting. Now, if you can't immediately press a button or see something blown up, the game is *boring.* If there is no immediate feedback or payoff, children will tune out.

Dr. Walt Larrimore, vice president of medical outreach at Focus on the Family, reminds us of how prevalent this problem is when he says,

"According to the Centers for Disease Control and Prevention (CDC) in 2002, 7 percent of children in the U.S. ages 6 to 11 had ADHD. They also reported that half of children in whom a diagnosis of ADHD was made also have a learning disability. They calculated that at least one million children have a learning disability without ADHD. The total number of children with at least one of these disorders was 2.6 million."[3]

One reason for the seeming increase in this disability is the practice of having formal education start way too young. In years past, kindergarten was a time for play and fun. Today, academic concepts are presented earlier and earlier, and teachers are pressured to prepare even the youngest tots for testing, which then determines the status and eventual funding of the school district. This early push cannot be healthy for the growing neurological system of the young child.

Another factor is that the environment and cultural dynamics of home is more inconsistent today. The child of yesteryear spent more time with adults and less with peers. Faced with a myriad of caregivers, children are now forced to deal with varying and often inconsistent patterns of expectations. Not knowing what to expect is frightening for any child. For the ADHD child, it can be disastrous and tragic.

So, how do you distinguish whether an issue is related to the maturity level of your child or is truly ADHD? We often try to dismiss our child's behavior by rationalizing that our child is young and immature. When my son would run around like a helicopter and seemed constitutionally unable to sit still for more than five seconds, I always reasoned that it was because he was a healthy, busy boy. But most parents seem to know in their hearts that something is not right long before it is confirmed by official or unofficial diagnosis. When we quiet ourselves and listen to God and our gut instead of the experts, we can usually get a good idea of what is happening with our child.

One mom who answered a survey for me shares, "It takes a long time to sort out the different issues that come with the situation you're addressing. We had to address it biblically, medically, educationally, and socially. I have to say that now that [my son] is eleven, things are coming together more and he's becoming a young man we can be proud of. I don't think we would have had the time to sort all of these things out without doing homeschooling."

Because we are with our child 24/7 as homeschoolers, we have the opportunity for observation, introspection, and education that other parents with similar children might not have.

Don't neglect the study of your child's temperament, personality, and learning style either. The more you learn about your child, the better you can teach him to understand himself. This is a tremendous legacy we can give to our challenging child—enough self-knowledge to allow him to learn the self-control necessary to lead a productive life.

Neurological or Naughty?

So the question remains: Is your child ADHD or not? One self-proclaimed hyperactive homeschooler gives us some perspective. Homeschooling author and advocate Israel Wayne, of Wisdom's Gate Publishing and *Homeschool Digest* magazine, tells us, "Knowing how to respond to hyperactivity is the real key. Learning the balance between knowing when to discipline, when to instruct, and when to just lighten up and laugh is the challenge facing parents of hyperactive children. When I did something outrageous or embarrassing, my mother would have to evaluate my motives. Was I being disobedient, disrespectful, inconsiderate, selfish, etc., or were my intentions pure?"[4]

My son, Daniel, has done some pretty bizarre things—like locking the cat in the bathroom or dropping the tadpole on the table from a great height. When asked for an explanation for his behavior, at the root was usually an issue of creativity or curiosity. In these instances, he wanted the thirsty cat to have a consistent water supply, and he wanted to see if he could make the tadpole's tail fall off.

What motive could your child possibly have for what he does? Why is he or she doing it? If it is curiosity, keep him asking questions and discovering. If it is to get attention, find out why they feel neglected. If it is meanness, what are the deepest issues of that child's heart?

Keep in mind that other physical or mental issues may share traits with ADHD. The child who has processing issues may seem to not pay attention because the act of trying to process the information is too difficult. Tuning out or spacing out, while appearing to be an attention issue, may be a defense against the difficulty faced due to the learning disability. Also look for physical causes, like hearing problems, vision disorders, sleep disorders, reactions to medicine, and depression or anxiety. These conditions may be at the root of the problem and often cause ADD-like symptoms.

Remember that kids at various stages of maturity exhibit some of these behaviors some of the time—even without a "disorder." Nearly every child has spaced out or checked out mentally while adults are talking to them. These incidents by themselves do not constitute a disability.

ADHD Solutions

THE ATTITUDE

Knowing and loving your child are the first steps. A change in your child's attitude may very well depend on a change in your own attitude.

• Praise, praise, praise. Change in your child starts with change in your heart. Because your child may have trouble controlling his behavior or impulses, he often receives a tremendous amount of negative attention. You might be appalled if you kept a tally of negative interactions as compared to positive interactions with your child. Praise every positive behavior, no matter how small. If you are to break out of a cycle of negativity that may have developed with your child, you must change your heart attitude and purpose to see the good and the positive in your child. Be specific in your praise. Rather than saying, "Good job!" say, "I appreciate the way you sat and looked at me and listened while I explained the assignment." (See chap. 7 for more ideas.)

• Keep your cool. If we want our children to learn to exercise self-control and to control their impulsive behavior, we must do the same.

When we lose control, it does not help the child. If your child cannot control himself, and then he sees you out of control, it may cause confusion and fear. What is needed is positive calmness on your part.

• Teach your child calming, positive self-talk skills. Don't allow him to say, "I'm dumb. I'm stupid. I'll never be able to do this." When facing a challenge, teach them to ask, "What do I do first? How do I solve this problem?" Show by praising small steps and by verbal reinforcement, "Bit-by-bit I can do it."

Dawns writes, "When my son was young, we tried to keep things from setting him off. Things like being chased or tickled would keep him going for hours. If we were going somewhere new, I would try to take him there a few days beforehand when it was quiet so that he could get a feel for the place and would not react so strongly to it when the day came for the event."

• Teach relaxation techniques, like deep breathing. Because my husband is a police officer, he has received training in what to do when he is under stress. We have taught our daughter to take deep breaths to calm herself when her frustration gets out of hand. When practiced calmly and regularly, it is very effective.

• Background music for some children is helpful to calm and focus them. Others find it too distracting when they are trying to read or relax. Experiment to find out which suits your child. Delores from Missouri notes, "Like David used harp music to soothe King Saul's nerves, we've tried to keep soothing music around."

• Tracy in Arkansas writes, "I start off in the mornings with a kid's exercise or dance video to help with excess energy. Then I always start teaching with my ADHD child and keep his session to twenty minutes if he is having a hard time focusing. I continue the twenty-minute sessions rotating with his brother until all of his work is done."

THE HOME

Helping an ADHD child experience success in daily home life is not unlike parenting any other kind of child. Yet parents of an attention-challenged child need to exercise extra diligence. Because these children tend to push the limits in all areas of life, your consistency and follow through will pay dividends in helping your child mature and manage his own life.

• For young children who are constantly going in cabinets, drawers, rooms, or storage areas, placing a red sticker indicates that the area is off limits, while a green sticker means it's OK.

• Have crates at the door for shoes and a reachable place to hang coats and jackets. Put a "to-go" box by the door for all the items you need to bring with you for the day, like movies to be returned or letters to be mailed.

• Develop a system to organize your child's bedroom and bathroom supplies to make it easy for him to be successful with his self-care needs and eliminate nagging.

• Have clear expectations of what you want your child to be responsible for in the home. Decide: What do I want him to do? How can I make it worth his while? How can I put it into a visual reminder system so I don't have to nag?

• Keep your child on task with charts. Give check-off charts or written checklists for schoolwork and daily responsibilities. Use Post-It notes and place reminders on backpacks or doors.

• Even though you are homeschooling, get ready for school the night before. Lay out clothes and needed items so the morning transitions go more smoothly.

• Use picture checklists for younger children. Draw or photograph the actual items to be remembered or done. Attach them to a board with Velcro or brads from the office supply store. As the item is done, the child takes it down and places it in a storage pocket.

Some excellent chore charts are available at
www.christianadhd.com/
structure.html.

THE BEHAVIOR

• As with every other area, find more positive things to say. Challenge yourself to say ten times more positive things than negative things.

• Delores in Missouri gave her son an interesting assignment. She writes, "He's always had Bible memory verses to practice his handwriting with and memorize at the same time as his spelling. I've tried to make his verses uplifting, positive ones since ADD people tend to internalize the negative, preachy ones (pessimism, discouragement, depression). Last year, he had twenty-five verses of joy and cheer to memorize! His outlook changed for the better—everybody noticed!"

• Make sure your child knows the expectations at home, while doing schoolwork, and away from home. Sit down with your child and work together to set goals and expectations. Both parents need to agree and need to be consistent from day to day.

• Frame your expectations in positive terms. For example, "In our family, we show respect for one another," instead of "Don't hit each other!" Post these somewhere around the house.

• Have a signal to your child when their behavior or attention is getting off track. It can be a one-word reminder, like "Focus" or "Settle." Deborah from California adds, "I also have her repeat everything I tell her to reinforce it in her mind. Often I write it down on a yellow sticker to keep near or to remind her of what we talked about."

• Have clearly defined consequences for breaking the rules. Be consistent, with no surprises for these children. Yelling "No!" does no good in the long run. Redirect the children to get them involved in more positive activities.

• Consequences can take several forms:

1. Physical punishment. We found it had little effect on our most challenging child and just made us feel guilty. Does it teach a better way to handle the issue?

2. Time-out, or removing the child from the situation to cool off. Make sure your child knows the parameters: where it is served

and for how long. If they get up, the time begins from 0. Make it boring and do not place them where there is a lot of stimulation. Have a practice session so they know what to expect. In our family we have the younger offenders serve their time-out with their nose on the wall. Whatever method you use, when the time-out is over, it's over. Don't harp on the misbehavior.

3. Grounding, which can take several forms. A younger child can be grounded and required to stay in the house. Older children can be grounded in the house, can be grounded from friends, or from use of the computer or telephone.

4. Natural consequences are very effective. For example, if a child stays up too late, they suffer the consequence of being tired the next day. If they spend their allowance on a toy that breaks in ten minutes, that was their choice. If their schoolwork part of the day is not completed, no other activities are allowed— no television, friends, phone calls, or computer play. This is a great way to learn responsibility, especially when the stakes are low. Don't be quick to jump in to rescue your child from their discomfort.

• Don't argue or engage in a discussion about the misbehavior. Give the consequence and end the discussion.

• Some families use a token economy, where the child earns or loses privileges based on agreed upon expectations. A chart is kept, and rewards or loss of privileges are dealt with no lecturing or nagging. (See an example of such a system in chap. 7.)

• A good martial arts class can work wonders for an ADHD child. It helps them to learn focus, concentration, and respect for others. We had all three of our girls in a program at one time, and they all made great strides in these areas. Other parents of ADHD children report that similar programs have become their child's passion and vehicle for learning self-control.

• Teach them calming and self-control techniques. If something is distracting them, challenge them to pretend that distraction is not happening. Make it a game, and it will strengthen their ability to attend.

When they are upset, teach them deep breathing to calm down. If they are frustrated, help them use their words to describe the frustration. Teach them to tolerate their negative feelings and irritations. For example, if your child complains that his knee hurts, respond by saying something like, "Let me read to you until it feels better." This teaches him to shift his focus from one thing to another, which is a valuable skill to learn.

• K in Illinois says, "Parents have to make major adjustments in thinking, especially when handling transitions and overstimulating situations with this child." This is an excellent reminder to prepare our child for changes and to avoid overtaxing them.

• Fiona from Virginia shares, "ADD kids like anything with a screen, so computer/TV/Gameboys are or can be used as a reward or taken away as a consequence. That being said, had I known then what I know now, I would have thrown everything with a square screen in the river. Well, maybe not the microwave. Also, there are just some days when the brain synapses aren't firing and then I know we have to step back and take a day off because her brain, for whatever reason, is fried. That's when I have to get off my type A soapbox and realize these are the reasons why I homeschool—so I can tweak our schedule to fit what's going on within the family."

THE STUDY AREA

• Keep the study area quiet and make sure the child is not seated near a window, door, air conditioner, or heater.

• Make a study carrel if more than one child is studying in the same room. We bought a trifold display board, and my daughter sits behind this white screen, which filters out the visual distractions of the room. My daughter also has a set of heavy-duty earphones (the kind used on a shooting range) to filter out noise while she concentrates.

• Keep the study area as uncluttered as possible. Sometimes I look at my own dining room table and say, "Oh, my, how did all that stuff get there?" While it is handy to fold laundry and write out checks while your child works, it also may be tremendously distracting for him.

• To minimize book and supply clutter, provide storage bins and boxes for books and supplies. Keep these under the table or otherwise out of sight when not in use. Teach your child to have only one subject out at a time and only the supplies needed at that time.

• Designate an area for completed work where your child can place materials that need to be checked or corrected.

• If practical, color-code the child's books and notebooks. For example, cover the math book in red paper and provide a red notebook specifically for math.

• Set aside five minutes at the beginning of the day to get organized for the day and ten minutes at the end of the day to clean up and put things away.

• While reading aloud, give your child something to handle, like Play-Doh, drawing materials, or even Legos. Sometimes giving the hands something to do helps the brain to attend.

• Help them learn to attend in small increments. For example, today read one page; tomorrow one and a half pages. Today do five math problems; tomorrow do seven. This builds up endurance slowly and without undue stress.

TIME MANAGEMENT

• Post a schedule for the day so the child knows what to expect. Children are comforted by knowing what happens next in the day and by a routine, as much as possible.

• Have a family calendar and check it daily with your child to prepare for events and meet responsibilities. If your child has an activity and it is written on the calendar, make every effort to make sure it happens. If a request is made at the last minute and it is not on the calendar, it usually won't happen. This helps your child learn to plan ahead.

• Give the child checklists of daily work and chores.

• Help the child plan long-term projects by plotting a schedule for piece-by-piece completion.

• Allow extra time to complete work, whether an assignment or a test.

• For some students, the use of a kitchen timer is motivational. Tell your student, "When it rings, you may play for ten minutes." For other students, it is a distraction. Experiment to see which works best for your child. We use it effectively to end dawdling at mealtime. I set the timer and tell them that when it rings, the meal has ended. The older children use it to control the amount of time they spend on the computer or watching television.

• Allow your child to take frequent breaks.

• Give your child a watch with alarms to remind him of managing his own responsibilities.

THE TEACHING

Eric Jensen presented the latest research on learning and the brain in his book *Teaching with the Brain in Mind*. In his discussion on getting the brain's attention, he reminds us that we don't have to have their attention 100 percent of the time. "Today, you can have students' attention 20-40 percent of the time and get terrific results. We know how to get attention: use contrast."[5] He suggests changes in location; use of color; different music; field trips; and energizing rituals, such as group clap, change in voice, bells or noisemakers. "Overall, you'll want to provide a rich balance of novelty and ritual. Novelty ensures attentional bias, and ritual ensures that there are predictable structures for low stress."[6]

How can we incorporate this into our homeschool?

• Utilize color. Use highlighters and colored index cards as study aids.

• Allow the child to use colored pens and markers.

• Draw colored borders around important material. Highlight key directions for the child.

• Allow your child to move around to different locations to work. He might work for a while at the table, then move to the dry erase board. Allow him to shift positions frequently. A child can learn while sitting, kneeling, sitting upside down, or even jumping.

• Give your child a variety of ways to respond to material, instead of just writing papers or filling in blanks. Let them give a demonstration or make a poster. Provide hands-on projects, homemade games, and field trips as much as possible.

• Get your child working on a computer or word processor as early as practical. Because the physical act of writing is often difficult for these children, this is a better way to encourage them to write.

• Sometimes the child can record work on a tape recorder. If an essay answer is required or if the child wants to tell a story, allow him to use this alternative method.

• Give him something to fiddle with while listening. Legos, Play-Doh, screwing screws into wood (for older children), hammering golf tees into styrofoam (for younger children), or drawing something are all great activities.

Beware of forgiving with the *blinks*—a term coined by author James Reisinger: "A blink occurs as the ADDer's attention involuntarily shifts focus from what is relevant to something irrelevant. This shift from a local situation (such as talking, reading, or working) to some other internal mental content (e.g., a thought, picture memory, or plan) blocks the local information."[7] As you are instructing your student to move from math to English and tell them to turn to page 14 in their English book, your child may have "blinked" at math time and literally not heard the second set of instructions.

What About Drugs?

Enter into the world of your child's frustration for a moment. Her life is full of demands and distractions. She finds it difficult to obey, even though she may desire to do so. It is torture for her to perform academically. Relating to peers may be taxing because others may not know what to make of her behavior.

If a medication could help her to cope in all these arenas, would you deny it? While not all parents of ADHD children choose to use medication, there is also a false belief circulating that a child who "uses drugs" at an early age will become a drug user later in life.

Dr. Bill Maier, psychologist in residence at Focus on the Family, says, "The belief that treating ADHD children with stimulant medication will lead to later drug abuse is absolutely, unequivocally false. It is based on rumor, gossip, and the deliberate spreading of misinformation. In fact, children who truly have the disorder and are not properly treated have a higher likelihood of abusing drugs and alcohol as teenagers and young adults."[8]

Conversely, beware of professionals who view medication as the be-all-end-all solution. The study of the mind is still an inexact science. Professionals may differ as to their recommendations, as evidenced by the experience of Zan Tyler. Author and homeschooling consultant, she had her child tested by two different Ph.D.'s. "The first learning specialist—a female—said, 'Your son is a motor mouth, hyperactive, and easily distractible.' She recommended Ritalin. The second learning specialist—a male—said, 'Your son is bright, energetic, and creative, a man's man at the age of five.' He did not recommend Ritalin. I don't think the thought even crossed his mind. What diametrically opposed ways of viewing the same child!"[9]

Field note about medications: Physicians cannot phone in prescriptions to the pharmacy for these medications. You must go to the office to pick up the script every time you need a refill. If he is willing to do so, you might supply your doctor with envelopes addressed to your pharmacy. When refill time comes, you merely call the doctor's office and have the written prescription placed in the mail.

Facing this issue was enormously difficult for us. After prayer and consultation with our Christian psychologist and family physician, we reasoned that committing to a trial of medication was not committing to a lifetime of use. Many children outgrow their need for medication. In our case, we use half the recommended dosage and we only administer it on school days. We have recently begun to ask her if she feels she needs the medication on any given day.

While the prospect of giving your child medication is daunting, think of it as a trial run. You don't *have* to continue. If it is not right for your child, you will know and can select another medication or choose to use environmental and behavioral strategies alone. You are your child's best expert and advocate.

The Bright Side

Among my daughter's many wonderful qualities is her understanding and empathy for others. Because she has been the struggling child in so many situations, her compassion for others has grown. She often will be the one to comfort another child who is sad or hurting in Sunday school. At home, she is quick to offer her love and affection.

Carol Barnier, author of *How to Get Your Child Off the Refrigerator and On to Learning,* is the mother of an ADHD child. She gives us this wonderful perspective: "When it comes to highly distractible children, we don't need to lower our expectations. We just need to accept that they need other methods of meeting them. In fact, we need to raise our expectations. We need to provide activity, challenge and discipline that match their level of energy and capability. We need to believe and share with our children the belief that God made them this way for a reason. There are amazing achievements they will be able to accomplish that the rest of us in this world wouldn't have the energy for. It is our job and privilege to find that glorious outcome for this special child."[10]

The longer I live with challenging children, the more I truly believe they are a privilege because we are all growing more than we would without the challenges. Our spiritual "muscles" are strengthened and our creativity is heightened as we find the best way to bring out the best in these children.

Among the many myths about ADHD children is that their future is bleak. To the contrary, there are many successful people with this disorder. One writer offers the following list: Ansel Adams, Charlotte and Emily Brontë, Salvador Dali, Emily Dickinson, Ralph Waldo Emerson, Benjamin Franklin, Robert Frost, Zsa Zsa Gabor, Bill Gates, John F. Kennedy, Abraham Lincoln, Mozart, Jack Nicholson, Eugene O'Neill, Elvis Presley, Joan Rivers, George Bernard Shaw, Sylvester Stallone, Vincent Van Gogh, Robin Williams, Tennessee Williams, and Frank Lloyd Wright.[11]

I would, basically, be happy to have my child among such company.

Some have said that challenging children also may be intensely spiritual. Perhaps this is because they have been prayed for and prayed about so much! Our daughter seems to have an open line to God and converses easily and freely with him in her prayer time. One of the real joys of raising this child is encouraging this openness with God. She knows that she can call on him at any time. Perhaps it is because she has seen me so often in my moments of weakness falling to my knees to beg for his strength! And he has not disappointed.

Will It Go Away?

Dr. Walt Larrimore from Focus on the Family says, "Some researchers believe that ADHD may, for many, be a lifelong condition. But what do the medical studies actually show? One review of nine studies prospectively followed groups of children with ADHD into adolescence or early adulthood. In one analysis, researchers demonstrated that ADHD symptoms do usually decrease over time—with the rate of the disorder dropping by about 50 percent every five years. Nevertheless, researchers found that between 22 to 85 percent of adolescents and 4 to 50 percent of adults that had ADHD in childhood continued to meet the criterion for its diagnosis. In other words, up to one-half of children with ADHD may carry it into their adult years."[12]

Given the pervasive nature of these difficulties, it becomes even more important to focus on self-management and coping skills. Whatever ways you can strengthen your child's ability to interact successfully with his world, you are giving him tools to take with him throughout life. With awareness, knowledge, and coping strategies, these children can live productive lives, pleasing to their maker.

Check out this delightful book by Carol Barnier: How to Get Your Child Off the Refrigerator and On to Learning *(Lynnwood, WA: Emerald Books, 2000). She shares her story about her son's ADHD and strategies she developed to help him learn and to help herself to see the gift in her child. The book gives tons of practical suggestions on incorporating movement into learning, using manipulatives, and making games. An extensive appendix contains ready-to-use reproducible resources for learning games and more. If you have a wiggly Willy, this book is for you!*

CHAPTER FIVE

Personality Clashes

Loving the Hard-to-Love Child

Character cannot be developed in peace and quiet. Only through experiences of trial and suffering can the soul be strengthened, vision be cleared, ambition insured, and success achieved.

—Helen Keller

As much as I try to be people oriented and laid back, I am driven by projects and accomplishments. One of my brood is my exact opposite. She thrives on being with people and has a very fluid approach to completing tasks. We butted heads for years over schoolwork and chores until I really began to see into her heart. I had to learn to value the beautiful way she looks at life and key into how to communicate with her to accomplish what needed to be done in everyday life.

Children within a family can be as diverse in personality styles, learning styles, and approaches to tasks as night and day. My husband and I joke that each of our children has a different father. Of course, with three of the four being adopted, they each have a different mother as well! Our children are as unique as can be, yet I have observed that even in families with exclusively biological children, they are each crafted in unique and wonderful ways.

> *Fiona in Virginia writes, "I have had a personality clash with one of my daughters. I have learned to step back, both literally and figuratively, when tempers flare because the anger feeds upon the situation and gets worse. If I stay calm and don't get into it with her, if I just walk away for a while and let things go, the whole situation becomes easier to deal with."*

Parents can learn a great deal from the study of temperaments and styles. This work often is spoken of regarding adults, especially in the workplace, but is equally applicable to children. With some understanding of these characteristics, we can learn to understand, relate to, and motivate our children in a way that makes sense to them and speaks to their hearts.

> *Dawna in California laments that the personality issues between her and her son are intensifying. "This has become an issue now that he is a teen. Mostly I tell him he is entitled to his opinion and he must obey and leave it at that."*

If you are having trouble gaining your child's cooperation, don't immediately assume it's a heart condition, a disability, or a disorder. In addition to the factors of readiness, age, learning differences and styles, or curriculum that doesn't fit, it is enormously helpful to have an understanding of temperaments and personality styles.

Personality/Temperament Types

Are you a sanguine, choleric, melancholy, or phlegmatic? Perhaps you are a lion, an otter, a golden retriever, or a beaver. Still another theory of personality refers to Lucy, Snoopy, Charlie Brown, or Linus. The descriptiveness of the names almost speak for themselves!

By the time children are two years of age, they have begun to fit a temperament category. Those of us who have experienced either terrible-twos or terrific-twos can attest to this! While the pure temperament characteristics will blur during the time children are maturing to adulthood, they still give the parent clues as to why children act the way they do.

LaHaye's Four Categories of Temperament

Tim and Beverly LaHaye authored some of the earliest works in this area.[1] More to the point for our purposes is an older work by Beverly LaHaye called *How to Develop Your Child's Temperament*.[2]

Kym, mom of eight, says she deals with personality clashes "on my knees."
She further states, "I choose to set it aside and concentrate on the schedule, on his learning, and on the tasks at hand. I usually feel that personality clashes indicate a need for me to spend more time with that child—to grow to love them more so the quirks and idiosyncrasies don't bother me as much."

*JW writes, "The personality clash is
that they are like I was when I was
growing up, or so I've been told. I have
had to face myself and take it to the
Lord. It is a painful and growing thing.
I must keep me in close check and
be the example of behavior
I know I should be. I live under
constant stress and cling to the cross
to get through."*

Sammy and Suzy Sanguine

The first category according to LaHaye is Sammy and Suzy Sanguine.[3] These children are superfriendly, like to talk, and possess a cheerful, winning smile. They need these winning characteristics because they also have a short interest span and flit from activity to activity.

These children are generally pleasant and eager to please, but may sometimes act without thinking. "They fully intend to be obedient and please, but they get swept away with curiosity or a change of environment. Although many times he may seem to be premeditatedly disobedient, he usually is just forgetting the past and engulfed in the present moment. He easily forgets the past punishments and does not consider the problems his disobedience may present him."[4]

Sanguines may have trouble with their schoolwork because of their restlessness. Unless they are taught to develop self-control, they may struggle with consistent study patterns. Our challenge with this type of child is to teach them consistent habits and self-discipline. While sanguine children are charming, that charm can be used to their detriment. They need great bunches of love, but they also need boundaries and accountability. On a personal note, my husband and I find that our sanguine daughter needs to be kept busy. If she is idle too long, she will find or create some mischief. We keep her engaged in productive pursuits, preferably those involving people, and she thrives. She recently began volunteering at our local hospital, and all the workers there love her for her sweet spirit and outgoing personality.

Chucky and Cindy Choleric

The next personality type is described by the LaHayes as Chucky and Cindy Choleric. You will recognize these children as two-year-olds. They have a strong will, a determined spirit, and a fierce determination to do things their way. When choleric children play with others, they have to be the boss. A play date with two cholerics will likely be a contest of wills!

The choleric has a will that must be broken, but care must be taken not to break the spirit. If these children commit themselves to God, they have the potential to be leaders with great influence.

On the downside, cholerics must guard their tongues, as they tend to use blunt, sarcastic speech. Because they are such hard drivers with an intense need to be in control, they should learn early to submit to God. A failure to learn this submission early will leave them on a course of reckless self-will.

Our challenge with these children is to direct them toward productive goals. Put them in charge of areas of their lives to help develop their leadership potential. While giving them responsibility, be sure to define the areas of responsibility because their tendency will be to try to push beyond them.

Beverly LaHaye says of the choleric, "His motto is, 'I can do it myself.'"[5] Make sure he grows up confident, but knowing that God is ultimately in charge.

We find that our choleric child is a tester. She is constantly pushing the boundaries of what is acceptable behavior. As a young child, she got more spankings than the rest and seemed the least affected by them! Our challenge is to mold her will but not break her spirit. We need to always make sure her heart is turned toward us but not accept any nonsense from her. It is a balancing act, but a rewarding one.

*Delores says her son is a tester, more so
in his younger years than now. "He's
one of those children Dr. James Dobson
in his* Strong-Willed Child *book says was
born with a cigar in his mouth."*

Milty and Molly Melancholy

The word *melancholy* evokes images of a brooding pessimist, and
that is a good starting point to describe this personality. These children
have deep rivers of talent as well as a tendency toward depression and
perfection. They are faithful friends, but may have trouble finding a mate
who will live up to their expectations. Creative, sensitive, and artistic,
they may get their feelings hurt easily and may allow themselves to feel
inferior to others. Be careful how you criticize them, as it may wound
them deeply.

Beverly LaHaye advises, "When left to his own ways, he will no
doubt grow up to become a gloomy, pessimistic, self-pitying individual.
Fortunately, God gave these children parents to teach them how to have
joy and thankfulness instead of gloom, a wholesome positive attitude
instead of a negative attitude, and a spirit of praise instead of
self-pity."[6]

Our challenge when these children are young is to help them recognize and develop their considerable talents. In a sensitive balancing act,
we must help them achieve, but not be overcome by their perfectionism
and self-absorption. Help them to set reasonable goals and to seek joy in
all areas of life.

While the melancholic children need a great deal of love and secu-
rity, they also need to learn to be self-sufficient. Encourage them to look
beyond themselves and let them experience small successes to build their
self-confidence. They must always know in the depths of their heart that
they are creations of great value to their Creator—and to you.

Peter and Polly Phlegmatic

The phlegmatic child is said to be the most enjoyable child to raise because they are not demanding of a mother's time. They are naturally quiet, easy-going, and calm, and love to watch what is going on around them. Because of this tendency to be a spectator, they may be slow to talk.

Because they are so easy-going, their weaknesses may be hard to recognize, but the parent must carefully monitor their lack of motivation. Parents should always be looking for ways to teach them to be perseverent.

Mrs. LaHaye warns, "As this temperament grows into the teen years, he may become uninvolved with his peer group and activities that would benefit him socially and spiritually. He needs to be encouraged to be a participant and not just a spectator. He will have much to offer society but will probably need a gentle push to get involved. It is very important that he learn responsibility during his growing years so that he can gain his freedom when he reaches adulthood."[7]

This is the type of child you may need to push and prod a bit. Encourage them to get involved and take chances. Find or create opportunities for them to explore their interests because they may not find them on their own. They need your consistent nudging in life, but prod them gently and lovingly.

Where do you see your child? Where do you see yourself? Conflicts arise when there are extreme differences in personality between parents and children. Choleric parents with a phlegmatic child will be frustrated unless they recognize how the child is bent and learn ways to motivate him. Similarly, a sanguine child will be a puzzle to melancholy parents. Why is she so happy all the time?

Getting a grasp of this information can help lead to family harmony and understanding.

Florence Littauer provides a current personality assessment. See a listing of all her personality-related products at www.classer vices.com/CS_Personalities.html.

For free personality assessments, do a Web search for personality styles. *You are likely to come up with inventories such as the Enneagram or Myers-Briggs Inventory.*

THE DiSC

Another helpful assessment tool is DiSC. Based on the 1928 work of William Moulton Marston and updated by Ken Blanchard and others, DiSC helps sort out the two orientations to our personalities: people-orientation or not people-orientation, and active or passive relationships. The four characteristics combine to make up the DiSC categories. Each style carries with it an intensity scale from low to high.

A free online DiSC assessment is available at www.ForestHill.org.

Active/Task-Oriented (Dominance Pattern)

These people are active in their relationships and are task-oriented. They get results, but also may be impatient and push others beyond their limits. They work well under pressure and are happiest when busy.

The downside of this forceful personality type is in relationships. Because they are always in a hurry and always in control, they find it hard to permit others to help them and may not be sensitive enough to those around them.

A homeschooling parent who is a high-D will run his home-school with an iron fist. If the children are not completely compliant and on board with the parent's system, everyone will experience frustration.

*Motivational speaker and writer Lou
Tice of the Pacific Institute asks, "Are
you a perfectionist? Do you know anyone who is? Let's talk about the drive to
be perfect and what it can cost you.
What is so bad about being good?
Nothing at all. But trying to be perfect
can cost you a lot in terms of mental
health and harmonious relationships.
You see, people who can mobilize
themselves in the face of tough problems are usually folks who don't worry
about being perfect. They are happy to
move ahead with a partial solution,
trusting that they will invent the rest as
they go along. Now, perfectionists will
try to tell you that their relentless standards drive them to levels of productivity and excellence that they could not
otherwise attain. But often just the
opposite is true. Perfectionists usually
accomplish less, because they waste so
much time paralyzed by fear of failure.
They will not start anything until they
know how to finish it without any
mishaps and that is a mistake."
(Winner's Circle Network)*

Active/People-Oriented (Influence Pattern)

People who are high-I combine the positive go-getter qualities of the
previous description but have a great rapport with people. They are true

leaders—ones who can motivate and generate enthusiasm in others, then feel confident enough to delegate and trust other people to carry out their vision.

On the negative side, this type of personality may be too trusting and may overdelegate to others. They have grand ideas but are not always good on follow-up. Their willingness to share their feelings and emotions may get them in trouble when they share too much.

High-I children will have a messy room because relationships are more important to them than stuff. Cleanliness distracts them from time to be with people.

The homeschooling parent who fits this description is a brilliant teacher in August—full of ideas and enthusiasm and on fire for homeschooling. If her brood does not totally take the ball and run with it, and if she does not follow and hold her children accountable, she may lose control. Children may be too young or too immature to see her vision and work with her to reach it.

Passive/People-Oriented (Steadiness Pattern)

I confess I am a high-S. I try to always keep my environment and those around me on a steady path. I'm dependable (most of the time), loyal, and I love to work hard. I pride myself on being a competent person, and I persist in my projects until they are complete.

I struggle with the fact that I don't feel right unless I am working. It's hard for me to relax, and being busy makes me feel more secure. Being frequently caught in the trap of busyness can cause my spiritual life to suffer.

My weak point as a homeschool teacher is that I have a hard time functioning in an unstable environment. (When is the life of a homeschooler truly stable?) I sometimes miss seizing the moment because I'm stuck on a project. Trying to keep everyone and everything in check has the potential to squelch the creativity of those around me.

Deborah from California writes of her daughter: "She is a lot like I was as a child, so I can see all of the mistakes I made then being made by her now, so I want to try to help her avoid all the pitfalls I had to endure. However, this is also frustrating because I sometimes feel like she should already know better, and I frustrate her with my own frustration. She really takes on whatever bad attitude I happen to have and amplifies it a hundred decibels. So I have to be very careful to be especially quiet and gentle in dealing with her. Proverbs 15:1 says that a quiet answer turns away wrath but grievous words stir up anger. And I believe that my grievous words stir up anger in me and in her."

Passive/Task-Oriented (Conscientious Pattern)

This is the kind of person you want handling your taxes and your legal matters. They are attentive to details, always check the fine points, and are always prepared. They make good decisions.

Have you heard someone say, "If you want it done right, do it yourself"? This statement best describes high-C people. They tend to want to keep everything under their control and are slow to trust others. They are not happy unless they know what everyone around them is doing and are confident that it is being done correctly!

The home teacher with these qualities may drive her more artistic children crazy! The perfectionist homeschooler may frustrate herself and those around her. Learning, like life, is not an exact science. It's more about relationships than checklists, and that may be frustrating for this person.

God made us each with strengths and weaknesses to complement one another. A high-S mom can help keep a dreamy high-I on target in reaching their goals—or can drive them crazy by insisting that their path to greatness be orderly! A high-D father can help a high-C child to take risks and grow. Awareness of these differences leads to respect and appreciation for the great variety of God's creation.

Tracy in Arkansas takes measures to avoid personality clashes. She writes, "I will sometimes take five or ten minutes on the treadmill to refocus or

*reorganize my strategy with my eight-
year-old. He is usually taking a five- or
ten-minute break outside or 'helping'
his brother or sister. A timer for them
takes me out of the picture enough to
prevent any major clashes."*

CAREY'S NINE CATEGORIES OF TEMPERAMENT

Dr. William B. Carey devised a series of categories to help us understand human behavior. His insightful book is called *Understanding Your
Child's Temperament.*[8]

In his schema, there are nine categories of temperament:

1. Activity

Children high in activity are social and energetic and run the risk of
being labeled hyperactive. Children low in activity are often slow to perform tasks and may be considered lazy.

To manage children who are high in activity, give them lots of physical activities and be tuned in to when they need to move around. These
children will not sit long for workbooks! Give them a chance to move
around and let off energy. Children who are low in activity might need
extra time to do tasks and should not be criticized for their slow speed.
The completion of a task, not the speed with which it is done, is what's
important. Using a timer that governs the amount of time required on
a task is a good, non-emotional reminder of time.

2. Regularity

Children high in regularity need a predictable routine, schedule, and
environment. Children with a lower need for regularity are more content to
go with the flow and aren't shaken up by changes in the day or schedule.

To manage children with a high need for regularity, always keep
them apprised of their schedule and activities. Let them know well in

advance when things will not go as planned. Children who have a low need for regularity can be helped by having set eating and sleeping times, set study and activity times. Help them to become more time-sensitive by giving rewards or praise for projects completed on time.

3. Initial reaction or approach/withdrawal

Children with strong initial reactions to situations can easily approach challenges and be bold. They make a rapid fit in new situations, but on the downside, they may be too quick to accept negative influences. Children low in this area tend to withdraw or are inhibited and slow to accept change. They may avoid situations that might lead to positive growth.

To manage children high in this category, be patient. Their initial positive responses to influences you might not appreciate may not last. Whatever the age, keep an eye on them in dangerous situations, and don't let their curiosity get them in trouble. For children low in this area, avoid pushing them too hard with new experiences. Teach them self-management skills and allow them time to adjust to new situations.

4. Adaptability

Children high in adaptability are easygoing but may be quick to accept negative influences, such as antisocial values. Children low in this area may have trouble adjusting to caregivers and may be considered difficult children, but they are less likely to accept negative influences.

To manage highly adaptive children, beware of their susceptibility to negative influence. Role-play what is expected before entering into new situations. Teach them to make their own decisions rather than going along with the crowd. For children low in adaptability, avoid requiring them to adapt all the time. When changes are to be made, arrange for the change to occur in stages, giving lots of advance warnings.

5. Intensity

High-intensity children may be perceived as abrasive or annoying. They let their needs be known and will tell you they are plenty unhappy when their needs are not met! Low-intensity children may have many needs, but they do not express their needs well.

To manage high-intensity children, avoid reacting to them with the same intensity. Sometimes when they are ballistic, it is sheer pleasure for them to see you go ballistic as well. Try to look past the exaggeration to read what is really going on and then react to the real need. Teach them anger management and self-calming strategies. With low-intensity children, don't mistake complaints as trivial. Take them seriously and try to discern their real need. Beware of equating the lack of intense feelings with the lack of *any* feelings. These children feel deeply. They just may not show it as much. Listen for clues and unspoken signs.

6. Mood

High-mood children may be excessively positive about a real problem, minimizing the significance. Low-mood children may be unpleasant to be around but may evoke more involvement from their caregivers because of concern for them.

For high-mood children, encourage their positive responses, but look out for situations where positive behavior may mask real pain. Don't let the mood of low-mood children make you feel guilty. Their mood is not your fault, and you can ignore their unfriendliness as much as possible—but deal with real distress. As these children get older, encourage them to be pleasant with people, no matter what their mood.

7. Persistence and attention span

High-persistence children are absorbed in their work and may ignore others, but they are also likely to be high achievers. Low-persistence children are less efficient and do not perform as expected. Parents should beware of mistaking this pattern for ADHD if the child functions well overall.

Highly persistent children need to be reminded that it's OK not to be perfect. Gently inform them when an activity is going on too long and assure them that leaving some things unfinished is OK. Low-persistence children may need help organizing tasks into short pieces with frequent breaks. Reward them for each step of completion, not their speed.

8. Distractibility

Children high in distractibility are easily distracted and probably were easy to soothe as infants. Children who are not easily distracted (low distractibility) may be unaware of signals or warnings from others because they are concentrating so hard. These children are lost in their work when it's time for dinner!

Managing the highly distractible child was covered in chapter 4. The key points are to eliminate or reduce stimuli and redirect them back to their work. Help them assume responsibility for themselves and praise them lavishly when tasks are completed. For the intensely concentrating child who is low in distractibility, don't assume it's disobedience if your child ignores interruptions. Use that nonemotional timer to signal when it is time to move to a new activity.

9. Sensitivity

Children high in sensitivity are more perceptive of their surroundings. These children may have had colic as infants. They may react strongly to minor events and are more sensitive to light, sound, and crowds. Children low in sensitivity love noise and crowds! Because they are at home in chaos, they may miss subtle cues from their surroundings.

To help highly sensitive children, avoid excess stimulation. Help them understand themselves. Help them see that sensitivity is a positive trait in this callous world. For children low in sensitivity, help them be aware of internal and external stimuli. Frequently ask, "What's going on here now?" Actively teach them clues to reading the facial expressions or body language of others.

Make a chart of the nine characteristics Carey described and observe your child for a few days. Where do you see high and low levels of these qualities? Observe him or her in different settings and in exposure to a variety of people. This understanding and sensitivity to them can help them understand themselves.

◆ ◆ ◆

Michelle J. in Wisconsin has this wise perspective: "I have been honest with my daughter at times, telling her that I have not always been the best example, but how I want to help teach her to be better because it is to her benefit. I am constantly in prayer about my own attitudes."

It requires intense prayer, wisdom, and observation on the part of the parent to discern if there is a problem or if it's an issue of temperament or personality style differences. I am convinced that some cases of overdiagnosed ADHD actually may be a failure to understand and appreciate temperament and personality issues. This is also true for learning styles, the subject of our next chapter.

CHAPTER SIX

Learning Styles

Does Your Teaching Style Mesh with Your Child's Learning Style?

> *It's time to stop teaching subjects.*
> *It's time to begin teaching children.*
>
> —Joyce Herzog

One of my best homeschooling investments has been a minitrampoline I purchased at Wal-Mart for twenty dollars. We use it for "bounce teaching."

Kids get bouncy at some point in the day. My youngest, age six, is bouncy most of the time. I have finally learned to work with the bounce rather than trying to squelch it.

How do we use this great tool? Any way that works. Today my son was doing a page of math that required him to list before and after numbers. For his last problem of the day, the "after" number was 67. I told him, "When you finish that problem, you have to go jump 67 times on the trampoline." He said, "Sure!" The page was finished and he was off to bounce!

We have bounced while reciting the alphabet, learning to skip count, and drilling with flash cards. Even the older children get into the action. When we are reviewing for a test, they bounce while I quiz them.

Think about all the ways you can put a little kinesthetic bounce into your schooling. What are some ways to combine movement and learning? To do so accomplishes covering some schoolwork *and* using some of that bundle of energy at the same time.

Learning Styles

Most of you have heard of the three basic learning styles: visual, auditory, and kinesthetic. Each refers to the brain's preferred way to take in information. Most people have a dominant style and reinforce it with lesser ones. Knowing your child's style can make a huge impact on his home education.

Tracy in Arkansas, who has homeschooled less than a year, tuned right in to these differences in her two sons. "Joshua's learning style is social interaction," she writes, "and I will allow him to share school-work activities with his siblings as much as possible. Philip is hands-on learning/action-oriented. I take as much of his learning off the page and into a game as possible."

A challenging child may be the one who has a different learning style from yours. Such a mismatch can create stress for both the child and teacher. Yet if we are equipped with this knowledge, we can adapt to whichever way the "twig is bent." If you want to help your child learn more effectively, try to discern whether he or she is a visual, auditory (also called verbal), or kinesthetic learner.

Visual Learner

How do visual learners learn? They must see things and watch them demonstrated. Some of the characteristics of visual learners are that they must write things down to remember them. They are good at remembering people's faces, but may forget their names. These children like to organize their thoughts by writing them and listing their problems. If they are required to listen a lot, they may tune out. A cluttered workbook page will frustrate them.

If you recognize this bent in your child, encourage his learning with these strategies:

- Give plenty of visual aids, such as maps, diagrams, and charts.
- Use colored markers to make flash cards and other memorization tools.
- Use highlighters to draw attention to important information. Teach the older children how to highlight as they read their textbooks.
- Let them draw pictures or diagrams while they listen. Teach them story mapping as an aid to comprehension. Expose older children to graphic organizers to help them organize information in a visual fashion.

> *Note: A graphic organizer is a visual way to organize information. It can be as simple as a circle in the middle with three or four more circles with spikes poking out. The main topic is placed in the circle and subtopics on the other spiked circles. For a selection of organizers, see* www.eduplace.com/graphic organizer/index.html.

- For math, use graph paper to help them keep columns in order. Highlight the operation sign to draw it to their attention.
- Make science and history colorful and memorable by exposing them to colorful pictures. Let them collect these pictures in a notebook and tell what they are about to demonstrate comprehension.
- Keep the school area colorful, but free from clutter. Visual learners are distracted by clutter and disorganization.

Whatever type of learner you have, remember that each is unique. Mary in Texas writes, "I am not on the schedule that the curriculum company recommends." This takes a great deal of stress off everyone. As long as your child is progressing, however slowly, he is learning.

AUDITORY (VERBAL) LEARNERS

Auditory or verbal learners learn through verbal instruction, either from others or self. They have an "ear" for music and can repeat words, directions, or stories that have been told to them. They learn perfectly well in a lecture setting and may enjoy listening to music while they study. They do not like being required to write excessively or take notes. One of my daughters is auditory, and we constantly battled over writing down assignments and reminders. "I don't need to write it, Mom," she would say to me. "I just remember things." And she was right.

Auditory children might benefit from tape recording what needs to be memorized. Tapes of math facts and books on tape can be listened to in the car. When teaching new concepts, this type of learner likes to dialogue and discuss. As much as possible, read out loud and give directions out loud.

Here are some strategies for promoting auditory learning:

- Talk with them all the time. It is amazing how much "accidental learning" takes place by having dedicated time to talk!
- Give tapes to listen to and educational videos to watch. They can learn almost anything this way.
- Allow them to be tested orally or to give oral reports about the material they have learned or use a fill-in-the-blank tape for review.
- Reach back into your memory for all the techniques you used to learn things. Can you remember the tune you used to learn the books of the Bible? How about the poem to learn the months of the year? These little tips from your own past are a precious gift of remembrance for your own child.

KINESTHETIC LEARNERS

My bouncy trampoline boy is a classic example of a kinesthetic learner. He learns by doing and by having his whole body involved in the subject material. This type of learner remembers best what they have done or seen. They love to work with their hands, whether building with blocks, using tools, or writing on a computer. The use of games to teach and solidify concepts is especially effective. These children do not respond well to workbooks, to reading assignments that are too long, or to being required to sit still for long periods of time.

Some teaching strategies for kinesthetic learners are:

- Do project work whenever possible for all subjects. Get creative and incorporate the hands-on component in spelling (using plastic letters) and math (using manipulatives) as well as other subjects.
- Allow him to type or give oral answers to exams.
- Use a big chalk or white board for practicing writing, spelling, math, or drawing.
- Use multi-sensory reading instruction. We painted a small box top with red paint and poured salt in it to allow our son to practice tracing his letters as he learned them. First he used his finger, then we moved to a popsicle stick.
- Let him bounce on the trampoline, bounce a basketball, clap his hands, or march around the room while practicing rote materials such as the alphabet, math facts, or multiplication tables.
- Use hands-on learning in every area of your curriculum, such as a puzzle map to learn geography facts.
- Rather than requiring papers or reports, let the child do dioramas or building projects to demonstrate mastery across the curriculum. Imagine role-playing Columbus landing in America, or Thomas Edison in his laboratory!

Barbara from Arizona shares her experience with hands-on learning: "I find with all three of the children, the more projects we do together, the better they respond. When we studied Egypt and Rome, we did dioramas, made costumes and made a meal for the family.

When we did Rome, we actually ate on a low table and laid on the floor. After the meal, the children displayed the things that they made and stood up in costume and talked about some aspect of what they learned. They always love it and it really cements the information in their heads."

K in Illinois uses this type of style as well and reminds us that it "requires a high level of creativity and can be quite exhausting."

One of our older daughters is a kinesthetic, and she simply could not grasp the concept of subtraction. "Where do those numbers go?" she would cry. We tried counting blocks and pennies, but nothing seemed to work. In desperation, I placed a line of masking tape on the floor and drew numbers on it. I had her jump forward on the line to add, and jump backward to subtract. This child needed to involve her whole body in the process of learning a new concept.

To help my son learn his sight words, I printed the words on cards and put them into a baggie with magnetic, plastic letters. He uses the refrigerator or a baking sheet to spell his sight words with the letters provided.

> *TouchMath is a wonderful tool for kinesthetic learners or those having difficulty making the transition from using concrete manipulatives, like blocks, to making mental calculations. Children learn specific touchpoints on the numbers 1 to 9 and use them to add, subtract, multiply and divide. Contact 1-800-888-9191 for more information.*

◆ ◆ ◆

The problem in the traditional setting is that "school" works best for the visual learner. The child writes down what is on the blackboard, processes it, and regurgitates it back on a test. What if your child's brain does not work that way? He or she will feel like a failure. We have the marvelous opportunity to give our children a way that suits their bent, to train them up in the way they should go.

Cynthia Tobias is a learning-style expert. She helps distinguish between learning style and learning disability in her book *The Way They Learn*.[1] In her comforting, down-to-earth style, she tells us, "Many students who are struggling in school simply have learning styles that are incompatible with the structure of the traditional classroom and academic demands. Sometimes concerned parents jump to a conclusion and believe their children may have learning disabilities or disorders of some kind because they lack success in school. To help their children succeed, parents can spend an inordinate amount of money and energy searching for programs and cures. What they need to do is take time to sort out how much of the problem might be attributable to an incompatibility of the child's learning style with the school's traditional method of teaching."[2]

Before calling in the experts, any parent would be wise to devote some serious time to this inquiry. As homeschoolers, we have the precious freedom to teach any way we want to teach. Why wouldn't we choose to do it in a way that makes sense to our child? Are we too stuck in the old molds of trying to duplicate traditional school at home that we forget the point of our instruction?

So what are you trying to do in your homeschool? Mrs. Tobias reminds us: "Sometimes we parents focus on how we would like our children to *act* more than what we want our children to *accomplish*. But if we focus more on *outcomes* and less on *methods*, we may find our children succeeding in ways that have never occurred to us."[3]

She further challenges us to always ask, "What's the point?" If you are dealing with a restless child and you need him to listen to you read aloud, let him sit on the floor or move around in ways that do not disrupt others. Some parents let children play with Play-Doh or Legos while listening to a story. If the child is listening and not disruptive and can demonstrate that he has been listening by being able to narrate back the point of the instruction, it doesn't matter if he is sitting or standing on his head!

How can the parent be certain the bouncing child has understood the concept? Mrs. Tobias suggests letting him explain it verbally or in written form. You may want to let him draw a picture, make a diorama, or utilize any of the other suggestions listed above for kinesthetic learners.

Do you ever have trouble getting your child to complete assignments? Mrs. Tobias suggests helping him break it up into smaller pieces and holding him accountable for one piece at a time. If a child can score 92 percent or higher on a lengthy worksheet, he only should be required to do as much of the assignment as needed to demonstrate that he has mastered the concept. Why do all forty problems in the workbook if the child knows how to do the work? I allow my children to do every second or third problem, and if these are accurate, they can skip the rest of the page. If they are not, it indicates that they need the extra work and are therefore required to do all the problems.

What about the child who won't stay on task for more than a few minutes? Mrs. Tobias suggests, "Provide him with some options. Decide what needs to be done, then offer one or two ways to do it. Let him switch ways in the middle if he wants to, and let him keep on the move whenever possible while doing the task. Insist he do only one thing at a time, even if he quickly switches from one task to another. Help him identify which method he is using each time he changes direction."[4]

For the child with wandering attention, he must be monitored to help him stay on task. With my daughter, the minute I would turn my gaze from her, she would be off task. In our early days of dealing with her difficulty, she required constant supervision and redirection. With practice and maturity, she is now able to work alone for short periods of time. We had to work up to longer periods of studying alone. I began by leaving her side for one minute. When I returned and she was still working, I would offer lavish praise. Next, I left for two minutes, and so on. Today she can focus for about fifteen minutes.

As much as we wish to be sensitive to our children's learning styles and needs of the moment, sometimes things must be done *our* way. I cannot allow my son, for example, to express his kinesthetic style by letting him play in the street. When there are non-negotiable situations like that, show respect to your child by telling him why he has to do it your way.

Want an easy to administer test for your child? It also contains an abundance of teaching tips for each style of learner.
The Concise Learning Styles
Assessment *by Jill J. Dixon, M.Ed.*
Available from:
Diagnostic Prescriptive Services
P. O. Box 5098
Savannah, GA 31414
www.diagnosticprescriptive.com

Just as with personality and temperaments, other writers have expressed related theories of learning. For example, Dr. Jeff Myers, associate professor of communication arts at Bryan College and president of the Myers Institute for Communication and Learning, theorizes that there are four learning styles.[5]

- An *activist* likes to learn in a group or a team. This type needs people to bounce ideas off of and experience things together. This person would do well in a co-op or doing project work with other students.

- A *reflector* must read, think, and observe before taking any action. They need time to process information and then have the opportunity to ask questions. Give these children plenty of time to digest information before requiring them to use it.

- A *theorist* wants to understand how things work, and they need to understand the theory of things. When they have the big picture, they can then devise action points to focus their learning. Give these children plenty of explanations and extra sources of reading and research if you want them to truly understand something.

- A *pragmatist* learns in real-life situations. They need to immediately implement what they have learned. Don't waste your time telling these children the theory behind something. Just show them how to use it!

Related to the topic of temperament discussed in chapter 5, children also have environmental preferences in learning. Have you noticed a particular time of day when your child is most productive? Some children are, by nature, early birds and others are night owls. Who says that school has to stop at three o'clock in the afternoon? Tricia from New Hampshire wrote, "School is in session whenever Mom is awake!"

Some children can concentrate better when they have something to eat or drink while learning. A glass of milk or something to munch on may help them concentrate. I once thought that this was indulgent until I realized it is not too far removed from my own habit of having a cup of coffee when I read, write, or have devotions.

Ask your child if he concentrates best in bright light or soft, dimmer light. Does he like to work at a desk, or does he prefer to sit on the couch or on the floor? In the winter, a few of mine argue over who gets to sit on the heat register in the living room while they read. They cover up with a light blanket and let the heat create a warm air bubble over them while they read. Cozy!

In all of this discussion, the key to grasp is the need to allow our children to learn through their primary learning style for success. If you know their modes, you can succeed with *any* curriculum by adapting it to the child. Trying to adapt the child to the curriculum will only lead to frustration for the student and the parent, although some curricula are better suited to certain learning styles.

I really like Joyce Herzog's approach to learning styles. She is an author and consultant to families with special-needs children and reminds us that God made two categories: male and female. "Another way of looking at [learning styles] is that all of these are evidence of our natural man. Our goal as Christians is to let Christ shine through us. The more we do that, the more the lines of natural personality, learning styles, and talents become fuzzy. Perhaps it is more important to identify ourselves with the nature of Christ and the gifts which are given to us by the Holy Spirit and to lead our children to do the same."[6]

I appreciate this reminder. As a young parent, I thought the universe revolved around my precious child. When discussing these special accommodations for our children, it seems to promote that kind of thinking. While you are creating optimal conditions for your child's learning, remember that the ultimate goal is a godly child. Don't cater so much to his whims and whimpers that he becomes spoiled and expects special treatment everywhere he goes. I see this with parents of challenging children who allow them to skip chores because they can't be bothered with mundane family participation when so much extra time is required for their studies. They still need to work and to contribute so that when they are grown, they will be productive members of society, not whiners who feel God gave them the short end of the stick.

Valuing the Mind

Each of us has a mind that is a tremendous gift from God. He has gifted each of us differently. I can write, but don't ask me to sing. As parents, we need to become aware of each child's gifting and encourage its use because children are each gifted in one way or another. If we believe that children are a gift from God, teaching them to value their giftings and to use them for his glory is good stewardship.

Many challenging children suffer from low self-esteem because they do not seem as smart as the other kids around them or they don't learn as quickly. While mentoring them through the process of learning to make the most of what the Lord has given them, we need to remind them of their worth as heirs of the kingdom. If they build their self-worth on something other than that, it will lead to disappointment.

I am a licensed attorney who practiced law for eight years before becoming a full-time mother. That transition and loss of identity was devastating. I learned the hard way that if my child has invested so much of his identity in what he does rather than in what he is, he will be shaken when life throws him the inevitable curve ball.

We all want our children to have a good education and to perhaps have a career and a comfortable income. Education is a large determinant of future income, but we must teach our children that money is not the only thing in life.

I live in DuPage County, Illinois, one of the ten wealthiest counties in the country. (So why do they let *us* live here?) Many parents here make considerable sacrifices to send their children to prestigious schools. Their children may enter college with aspirations of a fast-track, well-paying business career, but at the end of four years, God may have placed a new vision in their hearts. They may want to dedicate themselves to the eradication of urban poverty, or to eliminate animal testing by cosmetics companies, or do something really outrageous—like be a missionary!

It is true that the world needs businesspeople, but it also desperately needs those who will work for less pay for the causes of society. Is one type of work better or more valuable than another? A child can live a godly life and be self-sufficient on a modest salary or a generous one. It requires a fine balancing act to encourage children to work hard yet instill in them the understanding that the worth of a life doesn't have a dollar value.

It begins early on with modeling. Do you pressure your children so much to excel in their studies that they learn that this is the only important thing in life? Are you so focused on their disability that you neglect the nurture of their ability? Don't allow the current challenge of your child's situation to give you tunnel vision about his or her future. God has marvelous plans for this child—ones you may not have even considered.

The Pygmalion Effect

What do you really believe about your child? Deep in your heart, what feelings or thoughts do you have about his or her potential? What expectations do you have for them? Are they high, low, or do you have none? Coming to terms with these and making sure that your beliefs, thoughts, and feelings are positive is a powerful determinant of how your child will do in life.

The ancient writer Ovid told the mythological story of a sculptor named Pygmalion. He carved the ideal woman and then fell hopelessly in love with the statue. The goddess Venus brought the statue to life. The sculptor invested his expectations into this creature, and we do the same with our expectations.

Eliza Doolittle, the flower seller in *My Fair Lady*, undoubtedly saw little potential in her life. Professor Higgins saw through her poor self-concept and began to treat her differently. This fresh treatment led to a change of attitude and ultimately a change of heart.

This result is known as the Pygmalion Effect and is based on the 1940s work of researcher Robert K. Merton and social psychologist Robert Rosenthal.[7] They observed that when a teacher had high expectations for her students, those students performed well. The teacher who had low expectations got what she expected. More extensive research led these men to conclude that the most important factor in a person's success is what opinion that those in authority over him hold. In other words, what we expect from one another often turns out to be what we get from one another.

Consider the power of this concept. The way we relate to our children, whether positively or negatively, will directly influence their success in life. One note here: Although my remarks are directed more to parents of children who are simply experiencing roadblocks in learning, even parents of severely disabled children—children with profound physical disabilities and/or mental retardation—should understand that the expectations of parents are key determinants of whether or not children reach their true potential—whatever that may be. The key is to have positive, yet realistic, expectations. Our interactions with our children set up an expectation cycle. We form an expectation, we communicate that expectation (overtly or subtly), our expectation is matched by the child, and our expectation comes true. If our expectations are negative or nonexistent, we may get what we expect. Positive expectations can reap positive benefits.

We behave consistently with the way we believe. We cannot act in a way that is inconsistent with our beliefs. What we truly believe about others will affect the way we act toward them. The way we act will affect the performance of the other person, either negatively or positively. Essentially, our expectations become a self-fulfilling prophecy because we will treat others the way we believe them to be, and their behavior will meet our expectations.

Much depends upon attitude and approach. When I am cranky and short with my daughter when she struggles through a concept that she *should* know, a chain of events is set into motion. She picks up on my frustration and gets frustrated herself. She knows I am irritated with her, so she becomes irritated. What is needed is a cool head on my part and a gentle consistent approach with lots of praise.

How do we communicate our expectations?

1. One key is to create a positive climate. When we are verbally supportive, give positive nonverbal cues, and help our child set challenging but obtainable goals, we are setting the stage for success. The way we communicate through our tone of voice, eye contact, facial expressions, and body posture say far more than our words. In a negative climate, we are in a hurry or distracted and do not give children our full attention. We send negative nonverbal cues with our expressions, tone, or posture. In the worst of climates, we are verbally critical of our children's competence or potential.

2. We create expectations through the quality of our input. We spend extra time and share ideas with our children for whom we have positive expectations. We give them resources and let them have ownership of their work while standing by to offer support and assistance. We give negative input, however, when we don't provide children enough guidance or information to succeed, or when we wait too long to check on their progress. Students feel they are left to sink or swim, when we, in fact, have the power to throw them a life preserver.

3. We communicate our expectations by providing children with ways to demonstrate and show a positive output. We give them challenging assignments and provide opportunities for them to practice skills. We give them exposure and recognition for their work—displaying it, showing it to others, or otherwise giving them a forum in which

to shine. On the other hand, we discourage positive output when we limit the scope of their work, don't seek their opinion, and cut them off or don't listen to them when they are speaking.

4. Finally, the feedback we provide can express positive or negative expectations. When our expectations are positive, we give children gentle suggestions on how to improve their work, reinforce desirable behaviors with praise and recognition, and constantly reinforce our own belief in their ability to do better and succeed. When our expectations are negative, we are distracted and in a hurry when they seek to share with us, we criticize them as persons instead of focusing on the behavior, and we make negative generalizations and define them by their labels.

When children have a good attitude, they will approach their schoolwork with more confidence. I like to ask parents and children to do an attitude check. Some only need to do it once in a while; some need it every week. Personally, there are days when I need it every hour!

To assess children's attitudes, ask them to choose the following statements that best describe him or her:

1. ___ If I work hard, I will do well.   ___ I'm stupid.
2. ___ I can do things when I try.   ___ I can't do anything right.
3. ___ I do as well as other children.   ___ I'm the dumbest kid
                                                   around.
4. ___ I remember when I review.   ___ I can't remember anything.
5. ___ Math is OK.   ___ I'm terrible at math.
6. ___ I do well on tests when I study.   ___ I always do poorly on tests.
7. ___ I can do it.   ___ I give up easily.

As you discuss with them their answers to the above statements, try to discern if a low motivation for school is a matter of a lack of effort or a poor attitude. Then go to work on a solution.

If the problem is a lack of effort, work with them to implement some good work habits. If the problem is attitude, help them become aware of their negative thinking. Have them write down all their negative comments about themselves for a day to see how much bleak self-talk they have. At the end of the day, have them write a positive counterthought for each negative comment. Looking back on a day of small successes can encourage a child to try harder.

What about you? How do you truly view your child? Let's say your child has a learning disability. Examine for yourself the expectations you might have for this child.

Choose the statement that best reflects what you believe:

____ This child is lazy.   ____ This child appears lazy because he has been beaten down by his negative experiences.

____ This child lacks ambition.   ____ This child has the potential to develop. It is my job to help him recognize and develop this potential.

____ This child is not very bright.   ____ This child can show his ability by setting and reaching attainable goals that will build his self-confidence.

How is your attitude? Try keeping a little notebook for a few days. Make a tally mark for each time you and your child have a negative encounter. Make another mark for each positive encounter. At the end of the day, see where you stand. Are you taking advantage of the powerful potential of the Pygmalion Effect?

CHAPTER SEVEN

Discipline

How Do You Teach a Child Who Won't Listen to You?

A child's back must be made to bend, but not be broken.
He must be ruled, but not with a rod of iron.
His spirit must be conquered, but not crushed.

—Charles H. Spurgeon

Matthew did not want to agree to anything his parents suggested. When it was time to make his bed, he would lay on the floor and flail his arms and legs. At suppertime, he would whine over the menu selection so loudly that his father was forced to send him away from the table. (Later in the evening, his mother would usually make him a cheese sandwich, his favorite food.) When he turned kindergarten age, his mother was in a panic. How would she now teach a child who refused to listen to her?

Amanda was the first, long-awaited child of a family of four. She was doted upon and spoiled—cherished, but not disciplined.

When she turned eight, she began to pick up some attitudes and behaviors from other girls at Sunday school. Not wanting to dissuade her from attending class, her parents tolerated the behavior.

Today, at twelve, Amanda is out of control. She screams at her parents and refuses to comply with the simplest requests. Her parents are worried about how this child is affecting their other three children.

We cannot teach children who do not listen to us. A fundamental question is: What happened to turn the heart of that child away from his parents? Parents who struggle with discipline issues remember those golden baby days when parent and baby adored one another. When did this child suddenly decide, "From this day forward, I shall not listen?"

I have read numerous books about child discipline. Should we spank or not? How often? How hard? What kind of rules should children be required to follow?

It is painful for me to recall and recount my husband's and my own missteps in learning to discipline our children. We have made every mistake possible. At times we were too harsh. At times we were too lenient. Definitely, and most often, we were inconsistent. Our children suffered through our bumbling attempts at parenting. Generally, they are unscathed, yet I cannot escape the fact that some harm was done by our ineptitude.

On numerous occasions we have asked our children for forgiveness. They have learned that being an adult means being humble enough to repent of wrongdoing. They have repeatedly, and with great grace, forgiven us.

We have had to forgive ourselves for being less-than-perfect parents. We began with the unrealistic expectation of being superparents, but the Lord allowed us to be humbled by presenting us with challenges far beyond our human ability to fathom. We had to come before him in our brokenness and ask him to forgive us for trying to parent in our own strength.

Romans 8:1 encourages us: "Therefore, there is now no condemnation for those who are in Christ Jesus." We are free to fail. We are no longer under the law but are covered by the blood of God's grace. He forgives us in his mercy, and we must forgive ourselves. We must fail while still moving forward, not fearing failure, but learning from our mistakes and moving on.

By God's sure, tender mercy, we have been able to persevere. Seeking his forgiveness and the forgiveness of our children and ourselves, we have continued on, resting in the sure knowledge that "his compassions never fail. They are new every morning; great is your faithfulness" (Lam. 3:23).

Deborah in California is the mother of six children. In response to a survey of parents who deal with challenging children, she wrote a lengthy, heartwrenching description of what her life is like with her challenging child. The following is her response to my question, "What techniques or strategies do you use to discipline your child?"

We have tried everything! We have gone from Dr. Sears to Gary Ezzo to Rick Fugate to Michael Pearl to Tedd Tripp to Reb Bradley. I must have every child-training book there is. I will just tell you what happened yesterday with Hannah (mind you, I also have five others to train every day!).

She has to get up and get dressed, feed her bunny and her caterpillars, and put away the plastics from the dishwasher before breakfast. Well, she gets dressed, but begins to play with the baby. "Feed your animals!" Mom reminds, and on her way she finds the book she's been reading on the couch, and she lies down and begins to read. Mom can't see her, so she thinks she is feeding her animals. Twenty minutes later everyone else is done with their chores and are eating breakfast. "Hannah, it's not time to read; that comes later today. Your animals are hungry. Go feed them!" She gets up and goes outside to feed the animals. She gets the plantain leaves for her caterpillars, but it takes her twenty minutes because she is hunting for more caterpillars in the yard. Mom calls outside, "Hannah, are you done yet? You're going to miss breakfast!" She then brings the leaves in to her caterpillars and has to recount how many caterpillars she has and talk to them all and let them crawl around on her and see which ones have made their chrysalides yet. "Hannah, you need to go back out and feed your bunny. You get to play with the caterpillars after your schoolwork is done." She goes back outside and gets distracted with something else, and before you know it, she is riding her bike around the yard. Everyone is finished with breakfast and hard at work on their studies. Mom calls for her again, "Hannah, come and eat now or you won't get any breakfast." She replies, "I haven't fed the bunny yet!" Hurriedly she feeds the bunny and comes in. She has to get the cereal and milk back out. Oh yes, she hasn't put away her clean dishes yet, which is holding up her brother, who has to load the dirty ones. She finally does her dishes (everything she does seems to take more time than the normal person) and begins to eat. While she is eating, she sees that her younger brothers are playing a game, so she leaves the table to get involved with them and everything is left on the table. I come by and see her food and ask if she's done. Oh no, definitely not, she just started. So back to the table with her.

Then, comes the schoolwork. Bible is the first subject. She either reads her Bible or does a workbook page with coloring or activity. She has somehow misplaced the workbook and has to search for it. Then she finds it but has lost her pencil in the process. Pencil is found, but now where did she put that workbook. Oh yes, she had to go to the bathroom and left it in there. Bible done; on to math. Brothers are already finished with three or four subjects by now. She is at page one for the next four hours unless I sit with her for no distractions. Some days I can sit with her and some days I can't. The little ones need tending as well. Brother says, "You're only on math?" to which she flies into a rage and begins to yell at and hit brother. Mom has to step in and correct brother for his unkind words, to which he repents, and now she has to deal with Hannah. She needs to be disciplined for yelling and hitting. She is unrepentant. She rebels and becomes defiant and badmouths me. Now she is isolated in her room until she calms down. After twenty minutes (and a few spankings) she is still screaming at the top of her lungs (then come a few more spanks). Mom cannot speak to her until she calms down, and she cannot come out until Mom talks to her. Finally, hunger seizes her and she finds it best to be quiet. Mom comes to talk with her. She receives her discipline and may come out; however, she cannot eat lunch until at least her math is done. This starts a whole new episode. Mom has mercy and allows her a piece of toast while she's working. Hannah makes a discovery: she says, "If I don't look at what's next in my math book, then I can do it better. But if I look, then it looks like too much and I can't do it." "Great discovery, Hannah; let's try that from now on!"

The rest of her day was filled with schoolwork and chores and no free time because she used it all up in all of her distractions and discipline issues (which got worse)—and this was a comparatively good day. I can be completely consistent and still find myself in front of a distracted, unhappy child. I have taken privileges away, sent her to work with her father, given her more work, found anything and everything that is right about her and encouraged her, and I still feel that her heart remains unchanged.

A challenging child can bring any parent to their knees. How do we approach discipline? First, with an attitude of humility. Second, with the kind of respect for relationships exhibited by Jesus.

How did Jesus relate to people? He loved all kinds of people, but he didn't hesitate to point out their sin or lack of faith. He took time to listen to them and drew them close to himself. He forgave them. He saw the very best in them.

That is the heart of discipline. It's not about how and when to punish. It's about the relationship. Does that challenging child know he is loved? A powerful concept in relationships is that of the emotional bank account. We make deposits into our child's bank account by loving them unconditionally and building them up. We make withdrawals when we are harsh, distant, inconsistent, and uncaring. When things are tough in homeschooling, chances are the emotional bank accounts of both parent and child are dangerously low on resources.

Effective parenting and effective homeschooling are about relationships. How much of your interaction with your child is talking *at* them, such as giving instructions or making assignments? God is more concerned with how we learn to relate to each other than he is with whether our children become academic whizzes. What is most important is how we relate to God, how we relate to our children, and how our children relate to us.

Do your children really know that they are precious gifts from God? Have you told them? Psalm 127:3 tells us: "Sons are a heritage from the LORD, children a reward from him." What is our obligation with regard to that reward? Our job is to equip them with skills and to help them discern how God is going to use their gifts and talents. We need to help them see that God has a plan for their lives.

We must first draw them to us. When we are stressed out or our expectations are out of whack, we push them away because we can't deal with them. We can't be effective disciplers or discipliners of our children if we have pushed them so far away from us that they want nothing to do with us.

Do your children feel that you are constantly negative in your approach and disapproving of them? Perhaps you are justifiably taking issue with some aspect of their behavior or clothing. If that disapproval is not counterbalanced by some intense positive interaction, they may begin to feel that they can never measure up to your standards, and they may give up trying to please you. If they are resistant to your leadership, it may be because they feel they are a disappointment to you and can never measure up to your expectations. Do you really accept them? Can they feel that acceptance if the only thing they hear from you is criticism? If your approach and attitude are harsh and judgmental, their inclination to cooperate will be slim.

If you show constant disapproval of their thoughts, feelings, and thought processes, it will only drive them underground, and they will hide their true feelings from you. If they don't have your deep core acceptance, they'll seek it somewhere else—maybe in outrageous clothing or unhealthy friendships.

The Bible does indeed say that children are to *obey their parents* (Eph. 6:1–2), but a few lines later it advises fathers not to *provoke or exasperate their children* (Eph. 6:4). When Jesus interacted with people, he met them where they were. He did not say or imply, "I will love and accept you if you meet all my expectations and make me look good." Yet we often place that burden on our children and wonder why they don't communicate with us.

Our job is to *lovingly* train them to obey both God and us.

> *Clara in Miami has an ADHD child with language delays. She writes: "He is extremely strong-willed, but I found that the rod was counterproductive. I rarely use it now. By the grace of God, this one of my children has a strong sense of wanting to be pleasing. He will avoid eye contact when he doesn't want to do something, but if I look at him straight in the eye and have him hold my gaze, he does not defy it."*

At one point or another, I have driven each of my precious children away from me. My relationship with my special-needs child was so bad that I felt I didn't deserve to be a parent. My first teenager challenged me so mightily and I was so critical of her and burdened her with such unrealistic expectations that I nearly ruined our relationship. My second teenager was so strong-willed as a younger child that I nearly broke her spirit. Every time I fail to acknowledge the tender, sweet heart of my little boy I can almost see a section of it hardening off from me. If confession is good for the soul, my soul should be feeling awfully warmed right now.

What Kids Need

Consider the crucial responsibility we have to teach our children to submit to authority. I never learned this lesson as a child. I rebelled against my parents, against God, and against most authority figures in my life. How different my life would have been if I had learned early on that I will always be under some authority and had learned to adjust my behavior and expectations accordingly. I would have spared myself much pain, the same pain I wish to spare my own children.

And so we talk about this. We are all subject to God's authority. In the home, Mom is subject to Dad's authority, and the children are subject to our authority. But there is so much more.

At work the parent is subject to his bosses. Within the church we are subject to the pastors and elders. If we attend classes at a homeschool co-op, we are subject to our leaders.

Without an understanding of these clear lines of authority, children grow up thinking that someday they will be *free*. Because of a sin nature, they want to move that freedom closer and closer. They constantly challenge the boundaries, and will continue to do so throughout their adulthood as well.

When my husband and I teach parenting classes together, he uses the analogy of a football field. Our goal, as parents, is to get our children down the field to adulthood. The field they travel has boundaries. These are the non-negotiables in life—things like faith, respect, integrity, and honesty—that form the sides and ends of the field. As they travel down the field, they do have some latitude, as long as they stay within the boundaries.

*Tricia in New Hampshire has a son with
physical challenges, and she writes,
"We sometimes do behavior checks.
I'll stop what we're doing and ask my
son, 'How is your behavior right now?'
He'll think back over the past few*

minutes and answer truthfully. I'll ask for specifics, and he'll point out specifics. I'll praise him for his good behavior and consult with him about how his bad behavior must be improved. If needed, we'll review the consequences of continued bad behavior. I try to spend more time praising his good behavior and explaining what behavior is acceptable in new situations than disciplining for bad behavior."

In addition to being clear on the boundaries, children have physical needs, like food, clothing, nurture, and shelter. They also desire a sense of belonging—a feeling of some control over their world and some sense of freedom and fun.

They need to be loved and to feel that they matter. Many behavioral issues can be traced to a deficit in one of these areas. For example, a child who does not feel a sense of belonging may decide to affiliate with the "problem kids" who may welcome him as one of their own. Or the child who feels he has no power over his life may decide to be the class clown to gain attention. Can you see how these deficits figure in to these behaviors?

Look at life from your children's perspective. If they have learning issues, they may feel stupid or inadequate. If they have behavioral issues, they may not fully understand why they act the way they do. They may have social difficulties because they are different from other less challenging children. They may have emotional difficulties because of their issues, and these can become especially pronounced in adolescence. All of these challenges may lead to lowered self-esteem.

We must be careful not to allow them to define themselves by any label. Whatever their particular challenge, don't allow it to excuse certain behaviors, and don't let them feel sorry for themselves. The temptation to indulge in self-pity is always lurking in the background.

When faced with challenges, it is critical to have a strategy. Sit down with your spouse and discuss where the boundaries will be. For your family, what are the non-negotiables? They must do schoolwork. They must go to church. They must contribute to the family in some way. Remember to keep non-negotiables to a short list.

Next, decide what the negotiables are. They should keep their room clean. They should wear a coat when it is cold. Within reason, they have some free choice with regard to clothing, hair, and free-time activities.

How do you keep children running and maneuvering confidently down the field of life? If you have tried negative consequences with your challenging children, you may have found that they usually don't change behavior—they simply stop the behavior for the moment. Positive reinforcement and expectations will be longer lasting and have the greatest effect.

Negative consequences are what we traditionally think of as punishment. The child demonstrates an undesirable behavior, so he is presented with an uncomfortable consequence or he is removed from a positive situation. While this may help decrease negative behaviors, it does not strengthen or reinforce positive behaviors.

Positive reinforcement, on the other hand, increases the likelihood of positive behavior recurring. It is a pleasurable or rewarding response that can be used to strengthen an appropriate behavior. I believe positive reinforcement is more effective with challenging children because it counters the world of negativity inhabited by the child. Children are inundated with negative messages. They hear negative comments and have negative experiences regularly. Our mission is to create a positive atmosphere of love and acceptance to help them turn toward us and toward better behavior. So, how do we draw them closer?

Go for the Heart!

While doing some research on the Internet, I came across an interview with Howard Glasser who, along with Jennifer Easley, coauthored *Transforming the Difficult Child: The Nurtured Heart Approach.*[1] Upon reading the complete book, I was struck by the depth of understanding that these authors had about *my* children. Had the authors been lurking in my laundry room watching our family's interactions?

These authors begin by acknowledging that most parenting models or techniques work for the average child, but are less effective with the challenging child. The Nurtured Heart Approach, on the other hand, is not only for challenging children, it also can help the average child to do extremely well.

Have you noticed that the intense child thrives on our intense reactions? A small child who purposely pulls the cat's tail, after being told not to, seems almost gleeful at your emotional response. He seems to be thinking to himself, *Wow! See what I can make Mom do?*

I have a child for whom everything is *urgent*. When she talks to me about something, if she can get me caught up in the *urgency* of her request, she is more likely to have her request met. Having me swept away by her emotional torrent is extremely satisfying for her.

If you have a child who pushes your buttons and causes you to lose your cool easily, that child begins, in some perverse way, to enjoy the thrill of the reaction. Even if all they get are negative reactions, they still love the reaction and may provoke us to even higher levels of reaction. Essentially, they thrive on getting an emotional reaction from us. The more intense the child, the more they crave an intense reaction from us, positive or negative. Unfortunately, with challenging children it's usually negative! You can become stuck in a pattern of negativity because your reactions are interesting to them because they are intense. It creates a vicious cycle, and many times parents are puzzled as to how to break out of it.

What's a parent to do? When the child does something well, we need to give him an intense reaction. By catching the good, we can create powerful experiences of successes so he doesn't have to bother provoking our anger by acting negatively.

It is not enough to make ordinary positive remarks, like "Good job!" These are not intense enough to convince the challenging child that such a comment could be true. For parents who generally make positive comments to the child, this is particularly frustrating. Why doesn't the child believe them and take the comments to heart like other children seem to do?

This approach of giving our child intense positive reactions doesn't make the intensity of the child go away but helps them shift to using their intensity in positive ways. It will not break their will. It will teach them how to use it.

The authors of *Transforming the Difficult Child* talk about why video games are so seductive and such attention grabbers for children. "The reason is that their lives make total sense while they are engaged in the game."[2] The game is consistent and predictable because it involves acknowledgment and consequences. When something is done well or correctly, it is immediately rewarded. When something is done incorrectly, there are no bells and whistles or strong reactions. They take the consequence and move on in search of the positive affirmations of winning.

Contrast our interactions in heated situations. When the child sees there is more "payoff" for their bad behavior based on the intensity of our reactions, they go for the big payoff—that reaction! The authors put it this way: "Our challenging children are not out to get us. They are out to get our energy."[3]

To counteract this dynamic, the authors suggest we take three stands:

- Stand 1: "I refuse to get drawn into giving my child greater responses, more animation and other unintended 'payoffs' for negative behaviors. I won't accidentally foster failures and reward problems with my energy."
- Stand 2: "I resolve to purposefully create and nurture successes. I will relentlessly and strategically pull my child into a new pattern of success."
- Stand 3: "I have clear rules for my child and clear consequences when he or she breaks the rules. I resolve to give a true and effective consequence when a rule is broken."[4]

Our challenge is to prove to the child that they don't have to act out negatively to get our energy. The authors suggest using the following strategies:

Video Moments: Describe to children what you see them doing when they aren't doing anything wrong. This shows them that you care about the small aspects of their lives, makes them "visible" to you when they aren't misbehaving, and is received by the child as psychological nutrition. Give ten to twenty of these a day.

> *To a child calmly building with blocks,*
> *say, "You look pleased with what*
> *you have done. It seems you are*
> *really enjoying the building you're*
> *constructing." Other examples:*
> * *"I've noticed you've been using your*
> *best effort."*
> * *"I can tell you're upset, and*
> *I appreciate that you are handling your*
> *strong feelings so well."*
> * *"I noticed you are making a good*
> *effort to keep your room more orderly.*
> *Thanks!"*
> * *"I see you started on your home-*
> *work. Way to go!"*

Experiential Recognition: Provide children with a "freeze-frame" picture of success by giving them specific feedback for values, behaviors, or attitudes that you consider desirable. This recognition feeds their perception that they are valued for positive behaviors.

> *To a child who did not have a meltdown*
> *when a request to watch a movie was*
> *denied, say, "I can tell you were disap-*
> *pointed when I said no to your request.*
> *I see by the look on your face that*

you're mad, but I also see that you're
keeping that anger well under control.
Keep up the good work!"
Other examples:
- *"I'm happy you are doing your*
chores without being reminded."
- *"I appreciate your good manners.*
Thank you!"
- *"I like how you were honest when it*
would have been easier to lie. That
shows integrity."
- *"I appreciate that you accepted my*
'no' answer without fussing."

Experiential recognition helps to instill values. When children exhibit a characteristic or quality we want to encourage, we enhance the experience by recognizing their action and giving them a "freeze frame" picture of success.

Proactive Recognition: Give children recognition when they have not broken a rule. Children are often so accustomed to being chewed out for doing the wrong things that this technique fills their emotional tank for exhibiting good behavior. If there are specific household rules in effect, tie this recognition to the rules that have not been broken.

To the child who ruthlessly teases a
younger sibling, say, "Maria, I appreci-
ate the fact that you have not teased
Eva for the past half hour. Thanks for
showing her that consideration."
Other examples:
- *"I appreciate that you haven't used*
bad words today."

> • "You haven't been mean to the cat
> today. I appreciate that."
> • "I appreciate that you haven't been
> nagging me for treats before dinner."
> • "You haven't been aggressive to your
> sister today, and I appreciate that."

Creative Recognition: This strategy helps us to make requests of children in such a way that we are more likely to gain cooperation. If you're like me, the typical way is to shout out orders, as a drill instructor would do: "Hurry up!" Instead, when your child is dawdling about putting on shoes, say something like, "I guess you heard me. I appreciate that you stood up and are walking toward your shoes. Thank you for moving along when I asked you to, even though you may not be happy about it." The authors note that "this shifts the energy to a positive spin and conveys a message that every movement in the right direction is valued."[5]

> To a child who has a fit every night at
> homework time, say, "I see you're not
> happy about having to do homework.
> But I appreciate the fact that you have
> picked up the math book and have
> begun to look for your assigned page.
> Thanks for taking the first step."

Pick and choose your battles wisely. In the milliseconds that precede asking your child to perform a task, first ask yourself, "Is it worth the battle?" In other words, does this involve a principle, value, or matter where there is no compromise?

Oftentimes, parents find themselves on a power trip of sorts. When an order, no matter how nonessential, is not obeyed immediately, they make any level of resistance from the child an act of war. By acknowledging even the slightest attempt to comply, we defuse the situation and give the child credit for his efforts, however maddeningly small.

These techniques move our children to action while preserving our relationship. We are sending them high levels of positive emotional nutrition. These positive interactions are deposits into their emotional bank accounts. The reserves of love and high regard are the currency of good relationships. When children know they are loved, noticed, and appreciated; when their bank accounts are full; when they have had their quotient of positive emotional nutrition, then behavior change will begin.

In our family's experience, we have used these short, focused shots of attention along with recognition for positive steps with each of our children with great results. It may seem superficial to compliment something as small as promptly putting on socks, but the emotional impact of hearing a steady stream of positive comments throughout the day is powerful.

Many of us deal with children who have seemingly uncontrollable emotional outbursts. It is as if they are putting on an emotional fireworks exhibit. Our inclination may be to react with a similar level of emotional intensity. A better course is to tell the child, "The emotion you are feeling is understandable. The way you are choosing to *express* it, however, is inappropriate." This separates the child from the behavior. Along with our calm reaction, take the opportunity to teach your child some self-calming techniques. Encourage deep breathing or counting to ten. Always remember that you are dealing with a behavior, not a "problem child," and that with God's grace, behavior can be modified.

For more information on Transforming the Difficult Child, *go to* www.difficult child.com. *For another look at child training, check out the ministry of Michael and Debi Pearl at To Train Up a Child,*

*1000 Pearl Road, Pleasantville, TN
37033 (www.nogreaterjoy.org). They are
the authors of several books on the subject. Tedd Tripp has written a wonderful
book about connecting with your child
called* Shepherding a Child's Heart. *It is
available from Shepherd Press, P. O.
Box 24, Wapwallopen, PA 18660. JW
in California is the mother of nine children. She writes: "Rages and temper
troubles are a heart issue, but they hurt
and affect (infect too) every member of
the family, so the child is often isolated
until they can be honest about their
behavior and are willing to talk and
pray. I always ask them to get into the
Word and to talk to God about what is
going on. They are required to apologize
by saying, 'I was wrong for . . . Will
you forgive me?'"*

A Hard Question

Mothers, would *you* like to have *you* as a teacher every day? Would you be motivated or inspired by *you* for a mother? I still have days so filled with my own negative spirit that I wonder how anyone can stand me! The Lord has allowed me to see the damage caused by my critical spirit and has challenged me to examine and improve my attitude. With this came the sobering revelation that we can crush a child's spirit by our negative attitudes and excessive expectations.

Proverbs 14:1 says, "The wise woman builds her house, but with her own hands the foolish one tears her down." In my case, my "hands" are my critical spirit. All people deserve to be treated with dignity and respect, even in the height of disagreement. We don't have to make them *feel bad* to make them *act good*. We can say, "I love you, so I am concerned about . . ."

Conflict in any relationship is inevitable. It is how we deal with those conflicts that matters most, and what matters most is our attitude and approach. The more we accept that inevitability, the better we will be able to handle it when it comes. If we deny conflict, we are not teaching our children how to get along with others.

Another verse from Proverbs 14, verse 4, says, "Where there are no oxen, the manger is empty, but from the strength of an ox comes an abundant harvest." Oxen? What does this have to do with parenting? If you don't have oxen, you will have a clean manger, but you won't have the benefit of having strong oxen at your disposal. If you never had children (when your manger was clean), you would have less conflict in life, but you would never know the deep rewards and joys brought by the special reward of parenting. The presence of trials now means stronger relationships and better relationship skills in the future—for you and your child.

The way parents handle their attitude and approach is crucial. When we say, "Sit down and do your work," we are setting up a fight with a challenging child. If, instead we say, "Would you rather do your work now or later? If you wait until later, you won't be able to . . ." this gives the child a choice. Saying it lovingly tears down some of the barriers.

How do *we* feel when we are not treated with dignity and respect? I feel angry. Do you have an angry, uncooperative child? Knowing what you know now, how did it start?

Home Economy, or Token, Programs

When I am serious about improving my diet, the most effective way to do so is to write down everything I eat and provide a reward for compliance with my goals. This works because the mere act of self-monitoring helps to motivate me to change my behavior. The same is true of children and can be used effectively to manage problem behaviors.

Many books on discipline espouse an outcome-based approach and address the question, "How do I get my child to do what I want him to do and to stop doing what I don't want him to do?" The most common recommendation is to employ some type of home economy, or token, program. Let's examine the components and efficacy of such an approach.

The old adage rings true: If you don't know where you're going, just about any bus will get you there. In order to be successful, parents must first have a strategy. Take some time to write down your family vision and values. How, in a perfect world, would you like your family to look? Remember, athletes don't run a marathon the day after they decide to do so. From your values and vision flow desired behaviors—the ones that *really* matter in life.

Without a vision, we go through life rudderless and ineffective. Imagine an airplane flying to its destination. The navigator is consistently one degree off in his calculations. What's so significant about a single degree? Plenty. That flight could end up hundreds of miles from its desired destination. Seemingly small deviations from the values and vision we have for our family can lead to huge deviations in direction.

Delores from Missouri writes: "I learned to be firm, stand my ground when needed, but refuse to argue, and his privileges would go bye-bye! And he still had to do whatever was requested of him."

To begin, decide which positive behaviors you wish to see reinforced. Some examples might be getting up on time, taking a bath regularly, doing chores, or completing homework. Next, what are the negative behaviors you wish to deal with? In our home, recurring ones have been fighting, lying, and not doing chores.

Involve all your children and work together in establishing a system to address the issues you face. When our son was breaking his sister's toys, we said, "Dan, how would you like Clare to treat your toys? Then how should you treat *her* toys?" In these discussions always personalize the rules and allow them to see how their behavior impacts others.

Michelle in Wisconsin reminds us, "I find that my consistency is the biggest help in dealing with personality conflict and discipline issues. If I stay on whatever schedule/routine I have set up, it helps to reduce friction because she knows what is expected of her at any given time."

In a token system, the child is given points for positive behaviors and loses them for negative ones. Or each day might start fresh with an agreed-upon amount from which points are subtracted if undesired behaviors occur.

Next, develop a tracking system. We have used beans (described below) and charts with stars. Other parents have used tokens or have kept a tally of points for the day.

When all of the above is in place, choose rewards. Have a mutually agreed upon list of privileges and assign point values to each. Some ideas: going out for ice cream, playing video games, watching TV, having a sleepover, or renting a video.

The lessons learned by such a system are delayed gratification, motivation, and self-monitoring for the child to improve in problem areas.

When our oldest children were preteens, we wanted to impress upon them the connection that work is done in return for compensation. The Bible says, "If a man will not work, he shall not eat" (2 Thess. 3:10). We came up with a system whereby if one of the children did not do what was expected of them, they were not paid their allowance for the week. We tracked this by using dried beans in an egg carton. We called this system The Field Beans, and this is how it worked.

Each child started each day with ten beans. To maintain the ten beans each day, they had to do the following:

1. Brush teeth, wash up, get dressed, have hair neat—all without being told or nagged.
2. Be a table and kitchen helper, setting and clearing dishes for each meal.
3. Do an assigned morning chore and bedroom pick-up.
4. Do all schoolwork, homework, AWANA memorization, and music practice.
5. Keep room neat and clean (including *under* beds and furniture).
6. Keep laundry off the floor. Put away clean laundry when requested.
7. Have a quiet time of prayer and reading.
8. Do an afternoon/evening pick-up of house and bedroom.
9. Be kind to others at all times.
10. Have a pleasant attitude.

At the end of the week, each bean was worth five cents. If a child maintained all ten beans each day, at the end of the week he or she would earn $3.50 for the week. When the money was paid out each week, the children were required to give some to church and to save some. The rest could be spent as they saw fit.

This was a very motivating system for my growing children, who were at the ages when they wanted to have some money of their own. This gave them money, but it was tied to very specific expectations.

This system is flexible, and the parent can change the expectations as the need arises. It also can be used to work on attitudes, such as unkindness or harsh talk to one another. When a child knows they will lose a bean for being rude to a younger sibling, they often will think twice.

One of my children likes keeping records, and she really enjoyed being the accountant under this system. All of the children have since

grown too old for the system, but we are still very careful to tie allowances to expectations. Our token program inculcated early on the important connection between work and pay. A child does not get money
simply for existing. The family, in some respects, resembles a small corporation. Some members bring money into the corporation (usually
Mom and Dad), but each member of the corporation performs service
for the benefit of the corporation. In consideration of their service, they
receive a share of the profit in the form of allowances.

Household responsibilities are some of the "stuff" of family life. They
are also an opportunity to help create a sense of belonging. When you
require a child to pitch in and contribute, you are sending an unspoken
message that they are valued and needed.

The token system worked for my family. But let's look at a more
generic system you might want to incorporate in your routine.

First, lay the ground rules for behavior. Your child might earn points
for:

Absent behaviors
- No lying
- No disobeying
- No aggression or yelling
- No bad language or name calling
- No arguing or being disrespectful
- No teasing or bullying

Positive behaviors
- I was polite and respectful.
- I did as I was told.
- I handled my emotions with self-control.
- I had a positive attitude.
- I showed good manners.
- I showed responsibility.
- I was helpful when asked to do something.

Responsibilities
- I made my bed and cleaned my room.
- I did my schoolwork.

- I took care of pets.
- I helped at mealtimes.
- I took care of my hygiene.
- I did my reading for the day.

Assign a number of points to each of these categories. At the end of the week, give the child a choice of selected activities to spend their accumulated points. (An ADHD child may need to be reinforced more than once a week. Some parents purchase plastic tokens and pass them out at the end of each day. The child has a physical reward for their behavior, which is more immediate than waiting until the end of the week. They are then responsible for keeping them safe until they are redeemed.) The more elaborate activities will require more points. Some suggested rewards are:

- Television time
- Computer game time
- Video game time
- A movie rental
- A soda (great way to limit soda consumption!)
- A trip to the movie theater
- An extra treat
- Roller skating
- Skateboarding
- Bike riding
- Staying up one hour past bedtime on the weekend
- A trip to a dollar store
- Have a friend over to play
- Sleepover
- Fast-food dinner
- Ice cream shop
- Amusement park
- Pizza ordered in
- Parent does one of child's chores
- Spend night at friend's house
- Alone time with a parent

- Camp out in yard
- Telephone time
- Use of Internet
- Purchase of CD or movie

"But I Don't Feel Like Working!"

The best way to motivate children is with our unconditional love. Home economy and token systems are cute and interesting, but if we hope to gain our children's cooperation in life, they must know they are loved completely and totally. Ideally, we desire children who will obey out of love, not out of fear or the prospect of a reward.

Gary Chapman and Ross Campbell, authors of *The Five Love Languages of Children,* tell us:

> We need to fill our children's emotional tanks with unconditional love, because real love is always unconditional. Unconditional love is a full love that accepts and affirms a child for who he is, not for what he does. . . . Sadly, parents often display a love that is conditional; it depends on something other than their children just being. Conditional love is based on performance and is often associated with training techniques that offer gifts, rewards, and privileges to children who behave or perform in desired ways. Of course, it is necessary to train and/or discipline our children—but only after their emotional tanks have been filled. Those tanks can be filled with only one premium fuel: unconditional love. . . . Only unconditional love can prevent problems such as resentment, feelings of being unloved, guilt, fear, and insecurity. Only as we give our children unconditional love will we be able to deeply understand them and deal with their behaviors, whether good or bad.[6]

When we are certain in our own minds that our love for our children is unwavering, whether or not their room is cleaned, then we can begin the less intimate task of establishing consequences for their work behavior in the home.

The critical ingredient in teaching responsibility is to establish consequences for actions or lack of actions. Consequences may require some brainstorming on your part. There are two general types of consequences: withdrawing a privilege for a short period of time, or requiring restitution, that damage be repaid or undone in some way. The purpose of consequences is to help children learn, not to punish them. When they become adults, all of their actions will have consequences. The earlier they learn that fact, the greater ease they will experience in the transition to adulthood.

> *Karen has seven children, one of whom has a language-related disability. Her most effective consequence? "Isolation," she writes. "Time-out, doing homework away from his sisters, works quite well."*

When deciding on a consequence, ask:
- Is this consequence reasonable?
- Is it enforceable?
- Is it clearly related to the offense?
- Is it consistent with nurturing care, or is it motivated by anger, resentment, or retaliation?

Children often can be your best source of ideas for appropriate consequences. We had our first meeting when our oldest two were about four and five years old. At that time we were dealing with them slapping one another, leaving bikes out at night, and yelling. We asked the children what would be an appropriate response on our part to their behavior. They decided that if they left their bikes out, the bikes would be hung up in the rafters of the garage, well out of their reach, for three days. If they yelled unnecessarily, they would have to go to their room for ten minutes. If they slapped a sibling, they would serve a time-out. With the rules posted on a chart on the wall, we would merely point to the chart without comment when an infraction occurred, and the children would take their punishment. After all, it was *their* idea.

An interesting result of letting them brainstorm consequences is that children are often far tougher on themselves than adults would be. In our early discussions, they came up with harsher penalties than the ones we contemplated. For example:

- Not bringing dirty dishes to sink—they clean everyone's plates
- Toys left lying around—confiscated for a day
- Garbage not taken out—have to scrub cans outside
- Leave bike out at night—can't ride for three days
- Messy room—stay in room until it's cleaned
- Unnecessary yelling—go to a room where others won't be bothered

> *Dawna's son is autistic, dyslexic, and hyperactive. Here's how she handles discipline issues. "The first consequence is to lie on his bed for eight to ten minutes until the lemon timer goes off. (It is lemon because it is for sour behavior or sour words.) Then when his time is up, he has to come to me and tell me what he did wrong and why it is wrong. If he gives me trouble about going to lie down on his bed, I write '9:00 p.m.' on the white board, cross it out, and put '8:30 p.m.' for his adjusted bedtime."*

A consequence creates some discomfort for the child, providing an incentive to remember and obey. The above examples worked in our family. You know your child better than anyone else. What could you do to drive the point of responsible behavior home to them?

When children do something they have agreed they should not do, your calm response to them should be, "You have chosen to violate the agreement. Therefore, your consequence is. . . ." Without lecturing or talking them to death, you focus on the fact that they have made a choice.

When our children mess up, our tendency is to want to rescue them—take out the trash for them, do their stacked-up laundry, or excuse an assignment. This is short-sighted. We may be that child's hero for the moment, but long-term, we are teaching them that it is acceptable to not follow through and to drop the ball on their responsibilities.

Morris R. Schechtman, author of *Working without a Net,* writes about corporate dynamics and management, which has many applications to family life. He writes: "We don't throw our kids out on the street at an early age and expect them to grow [emotionally and intellectually] on their own; we don't give them complete freedom and no limits. We *manage* our relationships with kids"[7] (emphasis added).

Part of this "managing" inevitably involves conflict and confrontation, which many try to avoid, both at home and at work. But conflict and confrontation on the part of the parent can be used in a caring approach. If we can navigate these conflicts wisely at home, we will raise better employees and spouses who can manage the many conflicts of everyday life.

Schechtman lays out the difference between caring and uncaring: "In fact, an uncaring approach avoids conflict and confrontation. . . . The more we care, the more we should demand. . . . Let's return to our children analogy for a moment. When our kids start learning how to walk, they invariably bump into objects and fall down; they scream and cry in frustration. Should we as parents prevent this discomfort by picking them up and carrying them around? Is it a caring gesture to delay this natural and productive stage of growth? Of course not. The more growth we facilitate, the more we care."[8]

The author is also careful to remind us that there is a difference between *caretaking* and *caring for.* "Caretaking means that: You do things for people that they're perfectly capable of doing for themselves. The things you do persuade people that they are unable to solve their own problems; that anyone else would be better able to solve them. Caring for means that: You challenge people to be the best they can be. You tell them what they need to hear, not what they want to hear."[9]

The applications of this to parenting are many. To bail our children out is a form of caretaking. They will never grow to responsibility if we bail them out of every uncomfortable situation. It often takes only one incident of a forgotten jacket on a chilly day or having to wear messy clothes to youth group to cure forgetful behavior.

Another form of bailing them out is never letting them fail. Let them buy a toy (with their own money) that will fall apart in ten minutes. The next toy choice will be wiser. Let them choose candy that will disappear in a minute instead of a book that can be read and reread. That same child who asks for two dollars to go roller skating the next day can be gently reminded of his choice to enjoy the fleeting pleasure of the candy the day before.

Mumble, Mumble, Mumble

Do your children complain about chores or having to help in family life? When one of ours does, we remind them, "We serve each other in this family." Training our children to have a healthy, positive attitude toward work is one of the best life skills we can facilitate.

I shudder when I hear one of my children complaining about a simple request. Then sometimes I catch myself mumbling under my breath about having to do the same thing! If I grumble and complain about the task the Lord has given me of keeping a home, how can I expect my children to cheerfully assist in keeping the family afloat?

The same is true about work outside the home. If our children hear us continually complaining about our work, how will that influence their developing attitude toward work? They may begin to view it as something to be avoided or endured.

So much of life involves work. Whether we live in an urban area or on a farm—work is a way of life. My husband spent much of his childhood working on a farm. He recounts stories of entire seasons devoted to work—from sunup to sundown. Through this early acceptance of the fact that work is a part of life, he developed a positive, eager attitude toward work as an adult.

Challenge your child to look at the attitude they have when they work on something they love, such as a hobby or an anticipated project. Such an enjoyable pastime doesn't seem like work at all. So why not love what we do? If all of life involves work, we can model for our children the enjoyment of working. I heard an expression once that the secret to happiness is not to do what you love, but to love what you do. Do our children see this in Mom and Dad?

An admonition to cultivate a good work attitude is found in Colossians 3:23: "Whatever you do, work at it with all your heart, as working for the Lord, not for men." Our children's attitude toward work is really more important than the work itself. We can use work in our homes to teach our children positive work attitudes by training them with encouragement and example. Impress upon them that when we serve each other in the home, we are serving fellow members of Christ's kingdom.

Part of having a good attitude toward work is doing the work right the first time. I often see my children rushing through a job, and I remind them that if you don't have time to do it right the first time, you certainly don't have time to do it *over*.

Although we don't want to overburden our children with unrealistic expectations, there comes a time in a child's maturity when haphazard work is unacceptable. A two-year-old cannot be expected to keep their dresser drawers neat and tidy. Conversely, you can certainly expect this level of neatness from a ten-year-old. When the ten-year-old is held accountable for doing a job well the first time, they will carry that expectation over into a productive adult life.

Both in the home as a potential future parent and in the workplace, our children will be expected to perform with a good attitude and to complete tasks accurately the first time. By shaping this expectation in the home, we are preparing them for the reality of the workworld.

Contracts and Keeping on Track

As children get older, a contract can be an effective way of creating accountability. Parenting author Elizabeth Crary explains: "Contracts are used to clarify expectations and consequences. . . . Contracts can focus on household jobs, practicing music, studying, or personal behavior. Contracts spell out the effort each party provides, the benefits each person receives, and the consequences to each for lack of compliance. A contract is appropriate when both parties agree to the goal. The contract outlines how they will work together. Three steps in making a contract are: Clarify the purpose, decide who does what, and establish the benefits and consequences."[10]

What types of behaviors are appropriate for contracts? The test is this: Is the behavior that is the subject of the contract *observable, specific, demonstrable,* and *measurable?* If yes, then a contract might be effective. It would not be effective, for example, to have a contract with your child to exhibit "good behavior." Such a task is not specific enough. A more appropriate subject might be a contract to study for one hour a night in exchange for a sought-after privilege, such as using the car or having a sleepover.

In the past few years we have used contracts for pet care and for the purchase of musical instruments. Our pet agreement was as follows:

- We agreed to buy a guinea pig.
- The child agreed to feed the guinea pig each day and clean the cage once a week without being told.
- We agreed to not nag the child to take care of the pet.
- If the child consistently took care of the pet for one month, we agreed to take the child to the pet store to buy a special toy for the pet.
- If the child consistently failed to care for the pet, we reserved the right to find a new home for the pet.

In our home, this agreement worked beautifully for several pets. The last guinea pig we had was when the children were evidently beginning to tire of guinea pigs. He was not well cared for; therefore, according to the contract, we found him another home.

Another time we used a contract was when one of the children wanted to play the drums. We agreed to purchase a drum set as a birthday present. The child agreed to practice and play in the homeschool band. We agreed to remind the child only once a day to practice by means of her daily check-off list. She agreed to practice thirty minutes, four days per week, without complaining. If she kept the contract, she could keep the drums.

After the initial thrill of playing the drums wore off, we sold the drum set. There was no argument or disputing because the child knew what she had agreed to and was well aware of the consequences of not keeping her end of the bargain.

As children get older, contracts can be an effective way to manage their requests for greater freedom, such as borrowing the family car or taking outside jobs. Set realistic expectations. If they are too low, there is no sense of accomplishment for the child. If they are too high, they become discouraged. Find the motivating middle ground.

Parenting Pointers

Some additional parenting tips to help establish proper discipline within your home are:

• Pray with and for your children. Give them Scripture to plant in their souls to create self-talk about how much God loves them. Don't stop having devotions as they get older. Let them hear you praying for them.

• Focus on the positives of the seemingly negative. Does your child like to argue? He may be a budding attorney. Is he shy? He most likely is also sensitive and tenderhearted, and the world needs more tenderhearted people.

• Be a good listener. Paraphrase what your child has said and repeat it back to them.

• Sometimes it's good to simply be quiet and listen. Go into their rooms and sit on their beds (even if you can't stand the mess). Talk to them and listen to them.

- Build on their strengths. Encourage your children in their strong areas, such as the arts. Accomplishment in these areas can lead to improvement in academic areas due to increased concentration and motivation.

- For children with disabilities, strengthen their self-esteem by educating them about their disability. It can be a tremendous relief for them to learn that it's not all their "fault" that they struggle.

Finally, if discipline problems dissipate when you're not doing academic work, investigate the possibility of a neurological issue. What appears to be disobedience may instead be due to brain overload or processing issues. If undesirable behavior occurs consistently, even when doing chores or getting ready to go out for ice cream, it might be purely a discipline issue, requiring the use of some of the techniques we've discussed.

CHAPTER EIGHT

What about Mom, Marriage, and Siblings?

Managing Stress, Grief, and Discouragement

> *Pain is the megaphone through*
> *which God gets our attention.*
> —C. S. Lewis

M y husband bought me a DVD player for my last birthday. I am aware that it is 2004, but we are late to accept technology in our home. I enjoy it, and we are acquiring a nice collection of movies and slowly phasing out the VHS tapes.

One day, for no apparent reason, the machine stopped working. Although it was six months old, we had had the foresight to save the receipt. The merchant graciously gave me a completely new machine without batting an eye. I went home a happy consumer!

Some enter homeschooling with a consumer mentality. We listen to conference speakers telling us about the ten things a child should be doing by age twelve. Or the fifteen markers of maturity that should be in place by age fourteen. I pay close attention to the experts who tell me developmentally appropriate things to expect at various ages, but others left me with the sinking feeling that if my child was not measuring up, then I was a failure.

I shared this with my husband one day and told him, "I want my money back!"

"What do you mean?" he asked.

We were assured our kids would be spiritual giants if we only home-schooled them. We were promised there would be no teenage rebellion and that they would all go to Harvard. We were promised a rose gar-den—and ended up hacking our way through thistles and brambles.

In the beginning I believed that if I invested myself in this process, my children would (1) flourish academically, (2) be spiritual giants, and (3) never rebel against our authority. Be honest. Surely some of these thoughts also motivated you at one point—perhaps after hearing testi-monials at homeschooling conventions about all the merit scholars and fourteen-year-olds doing missionary work and being accepted to presti-gious colleges.

Well, guess what! I want my money back! I want to go to the home-schooling customer service center somewhere and make an exchange. I want to exchange my life full of challenges and struggles for a guaran-teed life. I figure if I put in all the time and energy required to do home-schooling, I want guaranteed results. I want a homeschooling Lake Wobegon existence: "Where the women are strong, the men are good looking, and all the children are above average."[1]

But God knows better, doesn't he? He gifted to us these exclusive children and allowed—and indeed ordained—the fruit we are seeing, or not seeing. The "success" we may have been led to expect by our home-school daydreaming may forever elude us. Perhaps God has other lessons we are supposed to be learning.

If the "results" of your homeschooling are not what you expected, remember that these children and this responsibility did not come from the Lord with a guarantee! If we do X, Y, and Z and do it faithfully and to his glory, the results are always in his hands—not ours.

Maybe you have the picture-perfect homeschool poster child. You are indeed blessed. You can be a beacon to the rest of us imperfect parents with imperfect children. Or perhaps you actually are paying a pretty high price to look good on the outside while hurting on the inside.

There are, in fact, a few guarantees in this endeavor. We are guaranteed that the Lord will walk beside us as we step out in faith each day. We are guaranteed that he will never leave us or forsake us in our time of challenge or need. We can rest in the guarantee that everything he allows into our lives is for his purposes.

While I may not be able to trade in my difficult life for an easier existence, I can rest in the assurance that I have all the guarantees I need, and I wouldn't exchange what he has given me for anything.

Each day I have the choice to survive or thrive. Even with God's assurance, some days are survival days. But if you spend more than a season in mere survival mode, take a hard look at your life. Don't just try to survive! Where is the victory there? We don't want to just stay alive— we want to make progress for the kingdom of God!

Psalm 127 tells us that our children are arrows (v. 4). We don't launch the arrows off willy-nilly and let them land where they will. Nor do we pull an arrow out of the quiver, shoot it at a blank wall, and then run over and draw a target around the arrow. We want to launch them in such a way that they will make an impact for God.

Our children are our arrows, and our work with them is our ministry for this season of life. The Lord allowed me to see that the way I deal with the weakest of his creation is my ministry. The work he has given me to do with children who are challenging speaks more than my "successes" with other children. The way I relate to and treat the least of them reflects his love to us. I don't always do a stellar job, believe me, but I have the blessed assurance in my heart that my family, with all its warts and imperfections, *is* my ministry. Like any ministry, we don't want to just survive. We want to shine for his glory.

The Emotional Journey

When you first realize or have confirmed the existence of a problem with your child, you go through predictable stages of grief. Like any loss, you are processing the loss of the prospect of enjoying the life of a normal child. I'd like to walk you through the stages I experienced. Maybe you can see yourself in the journey. More importantly, maybe the hope that shines so brightly at the end of the journey will encourage you.

Elizabeth Kübler-Ross was the author who developed these stages of grief through her experience of working with terminally ill patients.[2] Yet there are unmistakable parallels to working with challenging children.

DENIAL

After our daughter was evaluated by our local public school to see if she had a learning disability, we went to meet with the team that performed her evaluation. The experts at the school sat calmly around the conference table and told me that my precious child had a learning disability. I felt as if I had been punched in the stomach.

Present were a teacher, counselor, reading specialist, special-needs teacher, nurse, and the school principal. They all expressed their opinion about my child's disability. Then they handed me a thick sheaf of papers that documented their findings.

I initially denied that there was a problem. I couldn't/wouldn't believe that something was wrong. Maybe if we just waited another year. Maybe if we got another evaluation. At first my husband and I decided that reasonable minds could disagree. They had their opinion; we had ours. Still, in our hearts we felt uncomfortable with this conclusion.

Maybe she was just lazy, and we needed to work harder. The problem was, I couldn't imagine a sweeter child who tried harder than she. Yet despite her efforts, it just wasn't clicking.

And we couldn't blame it on the classroom teacher either, because I *was* the classroom teacher.

Finally I came to the point of intense sadness. I was paralyzed with it. I would sit and hold her and hearken back to the days when I had held and rocked her, blissfully unaware of the challenges that lay ahead.

ANGER

Then I became angry. I was mad at my daughter, mad at the school, and mad at the adoption agency for not preparing us for this (although none of it could have been predicted). Not all parents experience this anger as intensely as I did. For some, they are relieved to have confirmed what they have suspected for years.

As Christians, we must keep in mind what the Bible tells us in Ephesians 4:31: "Get rid of all bitterness, rage and anger, brawling and slander, along with every form of malice." We need to ask ourselves this question: Is our anger righteous? If we are angry with God, it is misdirected. If we are angry with a world that may not completely understand or accept a child who learns differently, we should take our anger and redirect the wasted energy into action that will help other children in our child's position.

In Mark 10:14, Jesus was indignant when the children were kept from him. He said, "Let the little children come to me, and do not hinder them, for the kingdom of God belongs to such as these." We too should be indignant at a system that will not help our child—or at a world that makes him feel odd.

Maybe you will become a teacher, therapist, or advocate for special-needs children based upon your experience. At the very least it will sensitize you to the struggles of other parents and prompt you to become an encourager.

GRIEF

Next came grief and the abandonment of dreams. I don't know what life holds for my child. She may never go to college, but I have settled in my heart that that would not be the end of the world.

As I read more about the strengths and weaknesses of children, the Holy Spirit allowed me to experience a mental shift. Children are a gift from the Lord. How dare I fail to appreciate the gift or to question the wisdom of the Giver!

My child may not go to Princeton, but her tender heart is leaning toward a service profession, such as nursing. What a blessing to have a child willing to serve the world rather than to only see what the world will give to her.

GUILT

Each stage was well-tinged with guilt. What did I do wrong? If only I had been a better parent, allowed less television, let her eat less white bread, made her eat more fish (brain food). What could I have done that I didn't? How did I fail? The list goes on. I experienced a tremendous amount of second-guessing, which was a waste of time and energy. There is an enormous difference of opinion as to what causes learning disabilities. Who was I to take total personal responsibility?

Some biological parents feel guilty because they fear the disorder was inherited from them. The feeling of responsibility reaches deep down and causes wrenching pain.

This constellation of emotions led me to feel overwhelmed and powerless. But it did not last long. Like any other new situation in life, I realized that knowledge is power. The more I learned about the disability, the more control I would have over my child's future and treatment options.

Also sprinkled into the emotional quagmire was a heaping dose of feeling inadequate. "How can I ever handle this?" I cried out to the Lord. James 1:2–6 spoke to me at this time: "Consider it pure joy, my brothers, whenever you face trials of many kinds, because you know that the testing of your faith develops perseverance. Perseverance must finish its work so that you may be mature and complete, not lacking anything. If any of you lacks wisdom, he should ask God, who gives generously to all without finding fault, and it will be given to him. But when he asks, he must believe and not doubt, because he who doubts is like a wave of the sea, blown and tossed by the wind."

I also took to heart Romans 12:12: "Be joyful in hope, *patient in affliction,* faithful in prayer" (emphasis added). If the Lord has allowed this affliction, my job is to be hopeful, patient, and faithful in prayer, relying on his wisdom and strength.

The experience has been a huge reminder to me that without Christ I am nothing but powerless.

ACCEPTANCE

The Lord has graciously allowed me ultimately to accept my assignment of being the parent of a special-needs child. Through all of life's trials, my husband and I wonder how people who do not know the Lord fathom the storms of existence. I rest in his strength and step out each day in faith. It is not easy, but he is faithful.

Deborah in California writes this of her challenging child: "My faith in God has increased as I have sought his face for the answers and help I need. I do not put my confidence in man, but lean wholly on God's strength. Some days I cry, though, and I have made it a point that when I am crying, to cry out to God. I also tell my daughter that when she is crying, to cry out to God. I can do what I can to try to change her outward behavior, but he's the only one who can change her heart. I take one day at a time and expect the best. Love hopes, endures, and perseveres. I don't have that kind of love, so I find it in looking at Jesus. He only did what his Father told him to do. I want that to be my prayer in dealing with my difficult child." Along with helping her daughter grow, this mom is growing as well. Perhaps this is how the Lord orchestrates things—for our growth and his glory.

Like any experience, one approaches homeschooling with dreams and a certain set of expectations. Our children may or may not meet them. Release those and let God unfold who he intends for them to truly be. Turn over your expectations to God. We can know for certain that he wants them to grow spiritually. Beyond that, beware of letting our expectations go ahead of what God has planned. Rather than become discouraged, we need to take that child from where she is to where God plans for her to arrive.

Sharon Hensley of Almaden Valley Christian School and author of *Home Schooling Children with Special Needs* reminds us in an interview in *The Old Schoolhouse Magazine*, "You cannot 'fix' your child's learning disability by homeschooling him/her, but you can give him/her a more appropriate learning experience. The more you accept the special needs of your child and enjoy who he/she is as a wonderful creation of God, the more true progress you will be able to make."[3]

Kym, mom of eight, whose son exhibited symptoms of autism after his two-year-old shots, writes, "I finally had to realize that I can't heal my child. This happened and regrets will not heal him, nor will my desiring it. So, we're here, and we handle reality. I just don't want to live in a dream or fantasy world. However, in the same breath I will say that I believe good things for my child—I know he can accomplish more, and I try to find the areas he excels in and get him involved there—singing, gymnastics, swimming, memorizing." This mother has been blessed with the gift of acceptance. She accepts where she is, with what she is dealing, and looks for the appropriate steps to take.

A lot of time and energy can be spent in asking God why our child is difficult or disabled. Margo Taylor wrote in *Discoveries* magazine:

> I used to tell myself that God had made them the way they were and I was to trust him. . . . I believe my children have learning disabilities because we live in an imperfect and decaying world. I don't think God created my children with learning disabilities, but I do believe that God filtered that part of my children through his love and allowed it. . . . You may have asked yourself, "Why?" My answer to this daunting question is "because you were chosen by God to be the parent and advocate for that child—a very hard and difficult assign-ment, which God knew you could handle (and needed to handle)." As parents, we must realize that we can't get our sig-nificance from our child—but only from God. You have chil=dren for what you can do for them, not what they can do for you.[4]

Am I Suited to the Task?

If homeschooling was easier for you with other children, you may have noticed the high level of commitment required to interact and work with a challenging child. These children especially need consistency. If you have been tremendously disorganized or nonmethodical, begin to pray about putting into place systems of organization and planning that will help you to manage the increased demand on your time.

Do not let what you perceive to be a homeschooling ideal dissuade you. It should be recognized for what it is—a homeschooling idol. There is a judgmental spirit among some in the Christian homeschooling community that exerts tremendous pressure to have your child look and act like all the other homeschooled kids. When they don't, the subtle and overt condemnation heaped upon you can be formidable. Michelle J., in a survey for this book, writes: "It is not always easy to admit to others that you have any 'problems' with your children or in homeschooling. It can make you feel like a failure as a Christian parent."

Homeschooling author and encourager Diana Johnson notes, "We expect faithful homeschooling to prevent sin or failure from ever entering our door. When it doesn't, we are quick to accuse ourselves."[5]

My friend Kym, mom of eight, writes, "One of the best ways I cope is not allowing myself to wallow in self-pity, negative thinking or talking, or with people who whine. That might sound harsh, but when mothering a severely special-needs child, sometimes the balance is so precarious that a shifting wind or word can blow me into negativity—and I just can't afford to live there. I've done it before, and had to pull myself up out of the deep abyss. No thanks. I'm not going there again. So I'm very, very careful who I associate with in these arenas." Kym has learned to set her face like flint to face the challenges before her and to guard her heart from those who would seek to dissuade her from her path.

We must let go of our unrealistic expectations for ourselves, our children, and for homeschooling. "Don't expect homeschooling to perfect your children. This is the lifework of Jesus Christ. Our efforts are a shoddy replacement at best."[6] Remember that our children are maturing spiritually, often right along with us. We must be open and receptive to the mighty work the Lord is planning to do though us and our imperfect family in our imperfect homeschool.

Emotional Survival

What makes the job of a homeschooling mom tough? We are called upon to be a mom-of-all-trades. We have to be all things to all people in our family, and there are constant demands on our time.

Short of sending the children to school or trading them in for another model, be realistic: are these things going to change in the near future?

Not likely, but you must pay some attention to how this lifestyle changes *you*.

Kym shares, "I used to ask my parents how to handle the emotional aspects of parenting my challenging child. Finally my dear father said, 'You do what you need to do.' That freed me. Yes, I could ask other moms for their input and advice. Yes, I could research and talk with experts. But when it came right down to it, God gave me this special child, and he promised to give me wisdom. So I ask for wisdom, don't lean on others so much, and I work through it. Dealing with reality is also better than living in the dream world. When he would misbehave, I'd daydream about putting him into a school rather than teaching him at home. Finally, I realized whether I put him in school or not, I had to deal with his behavior issues. Once I dealt with them, the desire to put him in school was gone." Kym has settled in her heart that she is doing what she is supposed to be doing for her child, and this has brought her great peace. Is it easy? No.

Because life is at times like a roller coaster, some of us may have learned to suppress our emotions. For the first several years, we probably loved homeschooling. Perhaps we then became a bit hard-hearted, a bit angry about all our responsibilities, a bit resentful of the constant demands on our time and energy. It's even worse when we get tunnel vision by measuring life by the results we are getting in our homeschool.

When we come to value the high test scores and the completed work-books instead of the process of being in this relationship with our children, we have lost our vision.

Life stress is normal. Normal people live in a normal range of stress. Have you felt during your homeschooling day that you're always on alert, living outside the bell curve of normalcy? Our feelings of high stress are caused by the million details involving children, meal preparation, laundry, and more. Add to this the stress and concern caused by a challenging child and you have a prescription for burnout!

Sherry Latson, doctoral researcher and contributor to the LDOnLine Web site, notes, "The results of my doctoral dissertation revealed that parents of children with learning disabilities had very elevated scores on the Parenting Stress Index, signifying that they perceived far more stress in their role as parents than did parents of children without learning problems."[7]

Being a homeschooling mom is a tough job, and your emotions are *normal.* Don't be harsh with yourself for having them. The challenge is to learn how to deal with them.

It's a law of physics that for every action there is an equal and opposite reaction. We live in a high stress state and must let down, often in the evenings or on weekends when our husbands are home and equally tired.

Because of our fatigue and the high stress we have endured, we might feel tired, detached, complacent, or apathetic. During our homeschooling day, we're alive, alert, energetic, and involved with our children, but the downward slope comes with annoying regularity when we live too long in this mode.

In effect, our lifestyle causes us to live on a biological roller coaster. We have the breathtaking highs, but *there are no highs without crashing into some lows.* I never understood this before, but knowing it has revolutionized the way I live. My expectation of myself was to always be upbeat and full of energy. When I could not sustain that level, due to the biological makeup that we all share as humans, I felt like a failure. I questioned why I couldn't do twenty projects at a time. It's because we're not made to operate that way.

When we are in that tired, detached state, we become horrible decision makers. We buy inappropriate curriculum and self-help books,
thinking they hold the magic answers to our predicament. When they
don't produce the desired results, that vicious cycle of frustration and
feelings of failure begins again.

This "shutting down" process is a biological response. When we are in
that state, it affects everyone around us. If we live with a spouse and kids,
they want to communicate. What do we want? We want to tune out!

It's easy to handle the highs of homeschooling. We relish them. We
brag about them. We cherish them. We tell Grandma about them. The
key to thriving in this lifestyle long-term is to look at how we can improve
the bottom half of that biological cycle in healthy ways.

Mary in Texas, whose son has a variety of physical challenges along
with ADD, writes, "First off, the most important thing to remember is
that God is with you, and he has made your child just the way that he
wants him or her to be. When times get tough, and they do, pray.
Sometimes, I just pray out loud. My kids look at me like I have lobsters
coming out of my ears when I just start praying very loudly, looking
upward, talking to the Lord. Hopefully, they will understand when they
get older."

Mary relies on prayer to lift her from the bottom end of the emotional roller coaster. Not everyone makes such a healthy choice. Because
we may be stuck in old patterns and habits, we try unhealthy ways to
make the lows less low. Some indulge in overeating, watch too much
television, or spend too much time on the phone as coping mechanisms
to avoid the inevitable. Others exercise too much or sleep too much.
Some of us find excuses to avoid being at home. We go to meetings or go
shopping excessively just to get out of the house.

It's not just marginal homeschoolers who are at risk for this bottoming-
out phenomenon. I have observed that those at greatest risk tend to be the
most dedicated, passionate, involved homeschoolers. The roller coaster that
rises the highest also has the most precipitous drops.

When we are at the bottom of this ride, we are the ones who are hurt the most. We cease to be the full persons we used to be. In a way, we lose some of ourselves.

As devoted, seasoned homeschoolers, we might be getting really good at teaching phonics or geometry, but we are starting to forget who we are and all the unique ways God created us to be. We become overinvested in the homeschooler role and underinvested in who we used to be—all the uniqueness, fullness, and brilliance of our interests, personalities, and talents that God so richly bestowed upon us.

It's the "USE2" syndrome. When I have a headache, I USE2 aspirin. But before I became such a busy momma, I USE2 ride my bike, I USE2 cross stitch, I USE2 read Irish literature and play Irish music on my flute and tinwhistle.

What is it that you "USE2" do before homeschooling? What do you do now when you're not homeschooling?

Not much, most moms would say. There are things you used to do all the time that you don't do anymore. Think about how this diminishes you. It impacts your sense of self, your personality, your spirituality, your interests, and your support system.

When we begin homeschooling, most of us are well-rounded. Parts of our "self" are hobbies, sports, church involvement, crafts, volunteering, friends, *and* homeschooling.

After a while, the world becomes small and our lives become narrowed to homeschooling. In homeschooling, we develop a singular sense of identity. We become synonymous with our role. When someone asks, "What do you do?" we say, "I'm a homeschooler."

When that role takes a downturn—when homeschooling is *hard*—our sense of self takes a downturn. We feel like a failure because the only thing that filled our basket has rolled out onto the ground. We feel vulnerable and emotionally at risk as we gaze into that empty basket. This causes some of us to excessively focus on what we cannot control, specifically *that challenging kid!*

The key to thriving in this endeavor is to focus on what we *can* control, such as:

- Our spirituality: the amount of time and energy we invest in developing our relationship with Christ
- Our integrity: the extent to which we live out our faith in all arenas of life
- Our passion: the degree to which we engage with the wonder of life

In the past, I would look at my husband and proclaim that he was overinvested in his work. The reality was that I was just as overinvested in homeschooling.

If we are ever to become thrivers—not just survivors—we need to get a grip on what we can and cannot control in life and prioritize our expenditures of time and energy accordingly. As the sense of control in our lives increases, the feeling of being burned out decreases. This is the key to emotional thriving and banishing burnout.

JW in California, mom of nine writes, "I could not survive without Jesus, church, friends, and gifts to myself, like a book, a latte, lunch out, or a new pen. Eating right is a must when possible. Soft background music to start our day is a peaceful way to start. It doesn't always work, but it is worth a try. I also work out at the gym. Focus is everything! If I focus on my discouragement, grief, marriage problems, the children's rages—I fail. If I focus on him, I will carry through to another day or the other side of a trial." JW has learned the hard way to attend to all aspects of her life to stay in balance. It's not selfish. It's self-nurture that frees us to love and nurture others, instead of hoarding the minimal reserves of energy we have.

DOWNTIME MANAGEMENT

Are you reactive in your life, handling each situation as it comes along, or are you proactive? For example, if your husband graces you with a dinner invitation and says, "Where do you want to eat?" do you say, "I don't care. You decide." What you need in this situation is a mental list of the places you have wanted to visit. It doesn't take a tremendous amount of mental energy to have ready a list of desired spots to visit.

In taking the small step of envisioning things to look forward to, our downtimes can be preplanned and personalized to the extent that we are comfortable taking some time off. Thinking a bit ahead like this puts oases in our schedules to anticipate. For example, your mental list might consist of Friday dinner at Old Country Buffet or a date with your husband to visit the new café downtown. There, was that so hard?

Make another mental list or actually jot down ideas for some special family outings, family trips, or family-days-out—and then *do them*. Look for free or inexpensive resources available in your community and use them to enrich your educational program.

Does this seem to lack spontaneity? Being tired, burned out, and incapable of a creative thought is *not* spontaneous! Waiting for spontaneity does not work either. Many times I have vowed to do more things with my family or as a couple when I felt more like it. The reality is that when I feel like doing nothing and then do nothing for 1,000 times, when the 1,001 time comes around, I still feel like doing nothing! We must plan our spontaneity. If we are prepared to have an outing or a bit of fun, it will help us keep our perspective on life.

Sometimes we say, "If only I felt better, I'd. . . ." Some of the if-onlys I have heard include taking up sewing, going to a support group meeting, going to a prayer meeting, or going on a retreat. However, because we usually put our needs last, we probably don't take time to do any of these things. The reality is that getting up and doing just one of these things will make us feel better.

Take the time now to make a list of four fun family things and four self-nurturing things that you would like to try. Pencil them in on your calendar, and then *do them*.

DECREASING LIFE'S PACE

We must slow down. Our society as a whole is obsessed with speed. Everything has to be done better and faster. We aspire to have our children be speed-readers and speed-learners. Yet reality with a child who has a disability is that learning is often a very slow process. Our desire for speed will only make us and our child frustrated.

Do you know how to tell if you have an unhealthy need for speed? When you stand by your microwave and mutter, "Hurry up!" We've equated speed with success. We have one-hour photos, one-hour dry cleaning, fast food that is free if it's not fast enough, speed-dial on our phones, and superfast Internet connections.

Does this speed really enhance our lives? When we hurry all the time, we lose perspective. We lose touch not only with those around us but also with ourselves.

Children equate love with time. It takes time to listen to our children, to our spouses, to our friends. It takes time and focus to listen to God.

I love technology, but I fantasize about what I have heard called *going Amish*—turning off all the electronics in our lives. These technological conveniences do something to us. We let the potential speed of technology determine our personal pace of life. Think about it. When someone e-mails or calls us, they request an answer *now*. Do we have no time for reflection and prayer about our decisions? Technology, if not used carefully, discourages us from letting a decision sit for a while. I have made more than my share of hasty decisions—usually with poor outcomes.

Where does the Bible say our strength lies? It's not in the speed of technology but "in quietness and trust" (Isa. 30:15). Although we may want a microwaved homeschool and parenting situation, what we really need is for our vision to simmer and steep.

Fiona from Virginia writes, "I make sure I recharge my batteries, and I don't feel guilty about doing it. If my cup is not full, I can't pour it out to others. Sometimes I just have to have a good cry. Above all, I need to remember to lean on God—something I forget, and usually when I need to do that the most."

Usually we forget to lean on God and fellowship with him when we are too busy. Can you slow down for God? He wants you to linger lovingly with him so he can fill your cup. Are you too busy?

Tending to the Physical

I avoided paying attention to my body for years. I was disconnected from my physical self due to some trauma I endured as a child. The Lord got my attention to tend to my physical needs by allowing me to inherit my family's heart disease. The word from my cardiologist was simple: "Do you want to live to see grandkids?"

When we are exhausted or sick, we can fulfill none of our missions in life. Health is like a rubber band. It stretches and snaps back. Yet if it is stretched too much or too long, it loses its elastic quality. It may become brittle and eventually break, resulting in sickness.

Part of being a woman is respecting the chemical balance within our bodies. When out of balance, our hormones, thyroid, nutrition, and more can cause fatigue and depression. If you are experiencing these symptoms, it would be worth your while to have a physical exam.

Our society is getting larger (obesity), sicker (diabetes and heart disease), and sleepier (lack of sleep). What are the things you can control? They are:

- exercise
- diet
- caffeine
- sleep

If any of these are out of balance, all of life will suffer.

One more note: Don't forget to laugh. Carrie in Arizona writes, "Never put laughter on the back burner no matter how hard or tough your day was." A merry heart can restore the balance we so sorely lack.

Avoid Overspending

Many homeschoolers buy more books and curriculum than needed. It feels so good to spend at the time, especially if it promises to make our life easier and more manageable. We convince ourselves that we would have a better homeschooling experience for our children if we just had _____. We end up focusing on things and technology and not on the relationship aspect of homeschooling. Our schooling problems don't improve—we just have more unused items to sort through, clean, and try to sell.

Instead of buying something to feel better, try *doing* something to feel better. It may seem hard to see beyond a present state of discouragement, but have the courage to ask the hard questions about your life right now: Will what I'm doing matter in ten years? What do I need more of in my life? What do I need less of? How can I make my life simpler?

MORE PRACTICAL POINTERS

1. Seek to understand your discouragement. You may have expected homeschooling or parenting to be easy. Give your expectations to God and let him carry your burden.

2. Discuss your discouragement with others similarly situated. Your support group composed mostly of overachievers may not be the place to go to look for such solace. Remember that God will always hear and understand better than anyone else. The worst thing to do is to go off alone. Lisa in Michigan reminds us, "We have had many ups and downs, joys and sorrows along the way. The joys have outweighed the sorrows, and homeschooling is something I will never regret, forget, or give up. I feel as homeschoolers we are truly one big family, and I would not want to see anyone give up this wonderful experience with their children." How can you tap into the family of homeschoolers? Look for support groups and Internet resources.

3. Never give up—on your child or yourself. When you look back on your life, you want to be able to say you have no regrets. Keep seeking, praying, and searching until you get a new perspective and a fresh vision. Don't go deeper in the hole of discouragement. Take some action, no matter how small, to climb out of the hole.

4. Accept imperfections, in yourself and others.

5. Learn to tolerate change. Life is always changing. Hold on to Christ and let the river flow.

6. Surrender your life to Christ! Release the ambitions you have for yourself or your child. It's his plan for your lives, not your own.

7. Plan for the things you do exercise control over. Make lists, draft plans, and write out schedules and menus so you don't stress out over everything.

8. How do you answer this question: Is it more important for you to see the temporal accomplishments of your child or his increase in Christlikeness? Be content to see godliness in yourself and your child. It's the only thing that really matters.

Ten Stressbusters for Homeschooling Moms

On a good day, breakfast happens with no major disasters. My three oldest kids help, then go off to wash up, brush teeth, get dressed, pick up their rooms and get ready for school.

While they're doing that, I get four-year-old Daniel washed and dressed and engage him in some activity. Puzzles, books, pictures, kid scissors, blocks, cubes, and many other things fill his "school box."

Soon enough, Daniel gets tired of it all and wanders off until I can cycle back to him later in the morning. Then Clare, Caitlin, Grace, and I go to the table to begin our work. I take turns working with each child individually while giving the other girls something to do independently. In between, I try to capture Daniel for some coloring or work with math manipulatives. Before we know it, it's about 11:30 a.m. and we break. They help me get lunch.

After lunch we rest for a few minutes and then complete the day's schoolwork. If it is an "outside" day, we prepare for that day's activity and try to get started on dinner. The rest time before lunch is usually the first time I have sat still since 5:30 or 6:00 a.m.

In the evenings, we read, attend a church or other activity, watch a little TV (yes, we do watch television!), or work on projects. The children then go to bed after giving thanks to God for a good day.

On a bad day, the youngest begins whining from the time he gets up. The older ones don't feel like doing school and have found the remote control and are watching TV when I emerge from my shower. They sulk and complain, but I turn off the TV, we fight our way through breakfast, and they finally arrive at the table for their time with me.

Meanwhile, the youngest is still whining.

My oldest daughter says she is too tired to do school and my second-oldest, strong-willed child informs me that she will not do school today. We struggle through each assignment, and by 10:30 a.m. I am exhausted.

We painfully get through the rest of the morning and fight all through lunch. I convince Daniel to take some quiet time in his room, and I go to finish up with the girls, but I hear some noises from his room. I check on him and find that he's strewn toys around the room, taken off all his clothes, gone to the bathroom all over his bed—and he's still whining.

The afternoon is a blur. The older girls are fighting and bickering, and my son is still whining. I scramble to finish their assignments and throw something together for supper. My husband arrives home. I greet him by saying, "What could be so bad about sending them to school?"

◆ ◆ ◆

We have both good days and bad days with predictable regularity. The difference now is that I have learned some ways to relieve the unending stress of my work with the children and carve out an oasis of sanity for myself.

Here are some suggestions for you to try as you employ your own stressbusters:

1. *Stop.* If you are about to explode from the stress of the moment, just stop whatever you are doing. Take a deep breath and look deeply into the faces of your children. Let go of whatever is making you crazy at that moment and focus on the blessings of your family. You may need to simply put the books away and go for a walk together to release the tension. Don't worry. The work will be there upon your return, but you will all have a renewed attitude.

2. *Slip into another gear.* When I was younger, I drove a stick shift. I could choose to go into high gear, or I could coast. We can make the same choices as homeschooling moms. When everyone is motivated, we work hard to accomplish our goals. When that motivation is waning, we have the choice to slip into another gear or to coast. If you're reading

textbooks, check out some library books on the topic and change your approach for a while. If you're doing too many workbooks, allow your children to give you their responses orally. Better yet, have them write something to incorporate all their grammar skills.

3. *Do something creative.* Mom, are there little things that you do that refresh you? Maybe you set the cross-stitch aside when the last baby arrived because your hands were simply too busy. Maybe you love to crochet or paint but feel guilty when you take the time to indulge your passion. The Lord made us with an infinite variety of creativity. Use the gifts he gave you to create something beautiful, homey, or quaint.

4. *Take humor breaks.* Have you laughed today? Sometimes I reflect on my day and I realize that I have not even cracked a giggle that day. Laughing is a great free stressbuster. Rent a silly movie and watch it with the kids. Ask the kids to tell you their latest jokes. Enter into the blessing of that moment and really laugh with them. You will grow closer and return to the task at hand refreshed.

5. *Do a reality check.* Are things really that bad? I was feeling awful about how our school year was going recently, and I began to reflect on all we had going for us: my marriage was thriving and growing, the children loved one another, we all had a passion for the Lord, and we were daily seeking to do his will for each of our lives. And by the way, we had read an awful lot of really good books and had made a substantial dent in our planned schoolwork. Things are probably not as bleak as you think.

6. *Practice patience.* I was the typical type A personality in my profession as an attorney. I drove myself and expected everyone around me to share my drive and ambition. When they did not, I became impatient. I realized I was imposing some of those same driven expectations on my husband and my children. Practicing patience requires both the willingness to accept those around us as they are and the willingness to enter into the sometimes chaos of life as it unfolds. Looking at others as precious gifts from God, made in his image, will automatically make you practice more patience with them, even when they don't meet your expectations. Living up to God's expectations is all that really matters anyway.

7. *Get physical!* As a homeschooling mom, doing some form of exercise is the best thing you can do for yourself. It relieves stress and puts you in a better mood. Take a walk—alone or with your family. Go to the park and actually play with the children. You all will feel better.

8. *Get enough sleep.* Are you staying up too late to watch television or read that book that has captured your imagination? Or, shudder the thought, are you burning the midnight oil to get chores done? Choose a bedtime for yourself as well as for your children. Other than the occasional deviation for a special event, your body and your mind will thank you for the gift of adequate rest.

9. *Sing!* There is music for every taste. Our family enjoys praise music, classical music, and Irish music. Someone once said you can't complain about your circumstances when you are busy singing praises. Although my voice is inadequate, it does not stop me from singing my praises unto the Lord.

10. *Pray.* The Lord will provide for every circumstance. He will meet every need. He is our hope and our salvation. He can take us through any trying situation—if we will let him have the steering wheel in our lives. When we delight in his law and meditate on his Word, we will be like the "tree planted by streams of water, which yields its fruit in season and whose leaf does not wither" (Ps. 1:3).

Reaching Out to Special-needs Families

Was it my imagination, or did we get fewer invitations to visit people's homes as the challenges of our children mounted? As the body of Christ, church friends and other friends need to be gracious to the parents of challenging children. When you invite me to your house, sometimes I cannot put a pretty face on our situation in time for the visit. Be patient with me. And my children. And don't judge too harshly. You never know when you might meet your own challenge.

Tracy in Arkansas knows this feeling of trepidation at venturing outside the family. She writes, "It can be very tense for all of us when we are out in public. We are all very self-conscious and keep to ourselves when out for family activities. We have to be feeling brave to go out with an autistic eight-year-old and a hyperactive five-year-old!"

In our own family there have been long stretches of time when we could not socialize because of the children's behavior. In one co-op we belonged to, my son bit three children during one meeting when he was in his biting phase. Thankfully, those times are gone! What can others do to reach out to families who parent challenging kids?

It is important to acknowledge the child. Don't pretend he isn't there or that his problems don't exist. Speak directly to the child and attempt to include him in what you are doing.

Consider giving some extra attention to the siblings of a challenging child. Chances are they share the burden at home. Bless them by giving them a new experience or a bit of fun. Think of the ways you can bless the family of a special-needs child, as they often feel quite alone for fear that people will not understand or accept them.

K in Illinois has a daughter who suffers from bipolar disorder with some aspects of ADHD and giftedness. She writes, "Parents can become very depleted, and have limited resources to re-energize. As parents, we don't share our daughter's disorder with anyone but very close friends (or 'anonymous' surveys) because it carries such a stigma and so many people are poorly educated about it, although it affects at least 1 percent of the population."

Jane Gambill, mother of a special-needs child, wrote an article for our state homeschooling publication in which she shares her thoughts and feelings about being the parent of a special-needs child. She writes:

> The gift of your time in prayer, on behalf of such a family
> or individual, is a special and worthy service. It is not, how-
> ever, the only area where one might minister to such a family.
> Ask God to give clear direction. He may want you to serve in
> other ways as well. Does he want your family to reach out to
> this family as a unit, or to one or more of the siblings? Do you
> have a daughter that God is directing to offer to go one after-
> noon a month and help the mother with cleaning, or baking a
> supply of home-baked goods for the freezer? Maybe one of

your children will be called to go and play or help with the special child occasionally, to free the mother to concentrate on the other children, or just to relax. Or maybe God will ask your family to offer to take this child into your home for a few hours a month.[8]

Homeschooling parents have already learned that their service to those in need is not in vain. Teach those around you how to help you so that they may know the same fulfillment. "I tell you the truth, whatever you did for one of the least of these brothers of mine, you did for me" (Matt. 25:40). If the people in your church or fellowship knew *how* to help you, they might be more likely to reach out. Surprisingly, they may be more blessed than those they seek to bless. They might just need some guidance from you as to how they might assist.

Support for Siblings

We often lean heavily on our other, normal children. The authors of the Focus on the Family book *Why A.D.H.D. Doesn't Mean Disaster* note, "Siblings are God's hands and feet in keeping their ADHD brothers and sisters walking a straight line, clear of trouble."[9] Sometimes we get so tired of fighting with the attention-challenged child that we place a large burden on the normal child. In our home, I have often relied too heavily on my other children.

Be careful! The other kids may not appear to "need" you as much, but don't be deceived. Not taking time to meet their needs could lead to their resentment of both the challenging child and of you. You are caught in a situation in which you are spending 80 percent of your time with 20 percent of your family. The siblings of a challenging child need your support and nurture as much if not more at times.

Deborah in California writes, "It takes my time away from the other children and the air of the home is filled with strife that they feel. Sometimes they are sad for her, and other times they are just frustrated with her. Sometimes we can't go somewhere we wanted to go because of her. On a positive note, there are many times we stop and pray and ask

God to take away all strife and to confuse the plans of the enemy over our family—this shows them where to go and what to do in future life situations."

It is critical to give your other children some special time and recognition. Here are some ideas for recognizing their contribution and sacrifice:

• Plan outings with each sibling alone. It can be as simple as going out for ice cream. My twelve-year-old and I started volunteering at the local animal shelter together. Through this she knows she will have 100 percent of mom at least a few hours a week, and we are doing something to help others.

• Recognize each child on a special day. Last Christmas my sister bought us a red special-day plate. Periodically, a child is chosen to eat off the special-day plate. At that meal, we each mention something we appreciate about the child.

• Include your other children in the educational program for the challenged child. They might help with drilling facts, tutoring, or reading aloud. We have had each of our older children partner with a younger child to do a computer program. For each day they work together, they fill in a square on a grid. When the grid is full (twenty-five days), we all go to the local candy store as a reward.

Don't blame the challenged child for not being able to do things, like going to amusement parks or museums. Karen in Illinois, mom of seven, writes, "The other children get aggravated because it is a tremendous time drain on the family. The little ones sometimes are deprived or even suffer because of it. We try to make up in other areas." In this instance, you might find someone to watch the child, or visit these types of attractions in short bursts.

Let your other children express their feeling to you about the challenging child. Ours are not allowed to disparage in front of each other, but we give them an opportunity to express negative feelings and frustrations privately with us. They have to let off steam sometimes, and we allow them the private space to do so.

Some parents have put one or more children in school while they worked with their challenging child. While this may work, it also may cause resentments, from either the child who gets to stay home or the child who has to go to school. Candace in Virginia writes, "I deal with some jealousy. My older son goes to public school and doesn't like it that my younger son stays home all day. However, he doesn't want to be homeschooled. He frequently says we favor D. There is a lot of conflict between the two and that causes a lot of stress on our family. D may have outbursts in public or act irrationally, so my older son never wants him to attend his school activities. Just going to a restaurant can be very stressful." The option of putting one child in school can be ideal if your non-challenging child is of preschool age. We have sent children to preschool at various points in our homeschooling. It provided a great break for the family and gave the little person some outside stimulation.

Your children may protest that the time and attention committed to the challenging child is not fair. The true test of fairness is whether all are getting what they individually need. It will not all be the same because they are each unique. Michelle J., who struggles with the oldest of her three children, writes, "My other children sometimes feel like she is getting away with doing less because I put off dealing with her to finish working with the younger two. They will at times mimic her attitudes." The reality is that it's *not* fair that one child takes up so much time and energy or appears to get special treatment. It's not fair, but it may be necessary. Gently remind your children that in the world, not everyone is treated the same, and remind them regularly of your love for them.

JW in California, mom of nine, writes, "[My challenging children] are very hard on their siblings, and sometimes it hurts deeply—to see it and to feel out of control to do anything about it. They are the example and it carries on into the little ones' behavior. My younger children who do not rage feel bad sometimes because I end up spending needless time working with problem kids. I try to keep a balance and be aware of their needs too." As long as we can keep some sense of balance, our other children will be OK, no matter how much they protest. They may even learn about self-sacrifice and service. That's a bonus aspect of your home curriculum!

Maintaining Your Marriage

I remember huge stretches of time when my husband and I were never alone. Every waking moment was consumed with the children. The first two were seventeen months apart, with the second one having a massive case of colic. Life was noisy, but joyous!

Over time my husband and I each began to nurse private hurts and slights. There was no energy for the niceties of relationships. We were a great parenting team, but we were forgetting what it was like to be a couple.

The challenges only increased. We had to learn conflict resolution and compassion for one another. Neither of us has an easy job, whether at home or in the workplace. Remembering to approach one another with gentleness and kindness has gone a long way in helping us weather the many storms of parenting. Along the way, we have agreed on certain principles:

• We must be united. Whether the issue is discipline or curriculum, we must be in communication with one another and present a united front to the children. When we have not been on the same page, the entire family has suffered. Deborah in California echoes this sentiment and writes of her challenging daughter: "When she was little we were not united. I thought he was too harsh; he thought I was too soft. We are still paying the price of that lack of unity. Our marriage suffered many onslaughts because of this challenge."

• We pray together and pray for each other. It has been incalculably significant to me to know that my husband prays for me and for our homeschooling. When we are having a particularly challenging day, the knowledge that he is praying for us can carry us through. Similarly, when he is in a stressful period at work, we communicate with one another what our prayer needs are. We know firsthand the power of prayer, for each other and for our children. As answers to prayer, the Lord has provided specific solutions to problems. Kym, mom of eight, writes of her husband: "We choose to pray together, almost daily, for our special child, for his healing and restoration, for our responses to him and for our ability to parent him." Regrettably, too often prayer is the last thing we try, instead of the first.

• We sneak small slices of time together. I can count on one hand the number of times we have been able to get away together for a weekend alone since we started our family. Despite the admonitions of the marriage experts to get away regularly, it is not always practical, especially when your children are challenging and your regular babysitter asks for combat pay! We have learned, however, to sneak small slices of time together. We both get up early to have coffee together almost every day. Because our oldest is now a very responsible fourteen-year-old, we sometimes leave her in charge while we go out to the bookstore together or to do the grocery shopping without all the children. These small slices of time, while they may seem insignificant, are ways for us to reconnect and remember that we are still a couple.

• We think of creative ways to stay in touch. My husband usually calls at least once during the day to see how things are going and to help deal with attitude problems. Knowing that he is going to call is often a great comfort to me. I know he cares and is there to help me deal with the day's challenges, as much as he can. We also sometimes e-mail things to each other during the day, especially if it is about something we do not want to share in front of the children. Feeling connected and supported is a great blessing.

• We find respite care. The parents of severely handicapped children routinely obtain respite care. You need a break from your challenging child as well. Maybe it's a weekend at Grandma's; maybe it's a day at a friend's house. Find a way to occasionally put some space between you and your child. You will come back refreshed and renewed.

While we may never truly understand why God allows us to have such challenging children, there is no doubt that he is at work in each and every situation to draw us closer to him and to each other. I want to close this chapter with Mary's story. Dealing with her son's physical and behavioral disabilities actually brought her to know the Lord. She writes:

> Initially when PJ was born, he had a heart murmur that
> kept him in the hospital. I was not a believer at that time. My

husband turned to the Lord in prayer. I was hurt and bitter and
refused to pray. My husband could not understand why
I felt that way. I felt at the time that God had not come
through for us because PJ was ill. It wasn't for a few more years
that I came to know the Lord. Meanwhile, my husband would
go to church on Sunday and take baby PJ, and I would stay
home. I guess you could say we were divided for a while. It
took about four years of my stubbornness and finally, in 1999,
I came to know the Lord and Savior, Jesus Christ. Now, some
years later, we are stressed, like most families, but we know we
are blessed. This is a season we are in right now. Our kids are
only this small once. I try to remember that. I enjoy them,
I laugh and play with them, and I just love them to death.
I thank Jesus each and every day for the wonderful gifts of
our children.

To which I say a hearty, "Amen!"

CHAPTER NINE

Planning a Program for the Challenging Learner

Some people see a closed door and turn away,
Others see a closed door, try the knob,
If it doesn't open, they turn away.
Still others see a closed door, try the knob,
If it doesn't open, they find a key.
If the key doesn't fit, they turn away.
A rare few see a closed door, try the knob,
If it doesn't open, they find a key,
If the key doesn't fit, they make one.

—Anonymous

I can't sing. I can't roller skate. I can't write poetry.

If I concentrated on all the things I do not know how to do, I would become discouraged. That vision of myself is one-dimensional.

God created me with many interesting facets. The ability to sing is not among them.

Sometimes I can imagine my precious child taking a similar inventory. She probably thinks, "I can't read well. I can't remember how to do math from day to day. I forget how to form my letters. I can't write."

The other side of her giftings-and-talents balance sheet is that she is a wonderful musician (violin), she is an amazing and intricately detailed storyteller, she can explain with great sophistication difficult science concepts, and she can tell great stories from history. Give her a project to work on that doesn't require much writing, and she is thrilled!

My job, as her teacher, is to work on strengthening her weaknesses *and* to use her considerable strengths. I love the approach of Joyce Herzog, author of *Learning in Spite of Labels,* who says, "Let's concentrate on our ables, not our labels!"[1]

Homeschooling, no matter how diligently and prayerfully practiced, will not solve all our problems. It will not cure a learning disability. Our goal as Christians should be to equip our children to live as productive believers. Scripture contains the true curriculum for life. The rest is mere knowledge.

I Don't Know If I Can Do This

When our child was diagnosed, my first inclination was to turn her over to the learning specialists. How could I possibly help her? I only knew how to reach and teach "normal" learners. When I threw up my arms and cried out "Help!" I realized that no perfect solution existed. I would have to do my research and create our own optimum, not perfect, program.

If you are considering homeschooling a child who learns differently, the first area to be addressed is your own doubt about your ability. Consider this: In a traditional school setting, your child struggles with a broad array of challenges. There are academics, attention, social issues, and environmental concerns—not to mention the likely complete lack of spiritual input. If your child is receiving "services," those services may only represent a small fraction of his day. Fleshing out the full picture, realize that after arming yourself with some knowledge about your challenge, you probably won't provide any *worse* an educational environment than your child is receiving in school now as a different learner.

On the positive side, imagine going to a dressmaker for a tailor-made garment. Although you may be an unusual size or shape, the dress fits your curves perfectly. Would this dress be of greater value to you than one pulled off the rack that all the other size twelves were wearing?

Homeschooling a challenging child is an opportunity to tailor a program to fit that child.

If you are fretting about the hours and hours of time that this will take out of your day, I have to be honest and say that homeschooling is quite time-consuming. After all, you are investing in human beings. However, it is a long recognized truth that it is much more efficient than classroom learning, from the teacher's perspective. A short period of one-on-one time is worth *hours* in the classroom. While the typical school day is six hours, many homeschoolers complete the bulk of their program in a few hours.

Being a good teacher has little to do with credentials either. Dr. Brian D. Ray, of the National Home Education Research Institute, reports, "Several studies found no relationship between parents' educational attainment and the academic achievement scores of their home-educated children in Texas, Alabama, Oklahoma, and nationwide."[2] Besides, it's not about *you*. It's about *the child*.

Remember, whether you think you can or you think you can't— you're right.

Start with Observation

In mapping an approach for your child, your first task is to intentionally observe your child. It may take some time and experimentation on your part. This will help you to organize and clarify what you know about your child. Laying this groundwork will be helpful if you seek help later because it will be an invaluable source of information to professionals. Even if you don't seek help, it will help you with your own planning.

When you live with a child every day, the dailiness of life, if you permit it, can be numbing. The child does A and you react with the predictable B. In making these observations, step back and don't intervene when you might normally do so. Record what is actually happening, not your feelings about it. Make short, frequent observations in a variety of settings.

Observe the child interacting with a variety of people: each parent, relatives, brothers or sisters, friends, strangers, and other teachers. Observe in a variety of settings: the child's bedroom, at the dinner table, doing schoolwork, watching TV, playing in the yard, playing at a friend's house, at Sunday school, in a public setting like a store or the library, at a party, during a visit to a relative's house, on a car trip, while dining out, or at a museum.

Pay particular attention to mealtime, bedtime, and schoolwork time. These are recurring situations in which your child probably has developed patterns of behavior. When you can look objectively, it will give you a glimpse into what is going on. The way a child acts when he is doing something stressful or challenging is a gold mine of information about your child. Let's look at one example of an observation:

> **Date:** 4-26-01
>
> **Location:** At the school table
>
> **Time:** 10:20 a.m.
>
> **Focus:** What happens when left alone to do work?
>
> **Purpose:** To assess follow-through
>
> **Observation:** After lengthy instruction and practice, Grace was left to do five math problems. She became obsessed with an itch on her leg. I checked it and there were no bites or sources of irritation. She spent six minutes crying and scratching, did one problem correctly, and then complained that her pencil wasn't sharp enough.
>
> **Thoughts:** She can't tune out her minor physical irritations or sensations.

When I brought this observation to one of her evaluations, it was a clear indicator that her internal distractions were so intense that they kept her from focusing on anything outside of herself. It also indicated that she still needed someone right at her side whenever she was called upon to do anything academic.

Here is a suggested form for your own observations:

Observation Log

Date

Place

Time

Focus

Purpose

Observation

Thoughts

Armed with a notebook full of observations such as the example above, you will have a wealth of information to present to a mental health professional or evaluator, should you choose to consult. Even if you don't use an outside evaluator, you can use this information to make decisions about techniques to help your child. In the instance above, I took this observation and researched alternative ways for her to respond to her math problems. We started a program called TouchMath (see resource section), we used a trampoline on which she could hop while adding numbers, and we put a large number line on the floor for her to move ahead (add) and back (subtract).

If your observations do not yield a clear picture of your challenges, take more extensive notes over a longer period of time. It is a critical investment in learning how to tailor that dress to perfectly fit your child.

One-Size-Fits-None

I fantasize about going to the learning disabilities catalog and ordering the complete third grade curriculum. Guess what? It doesn't exist. Most parents end up pulling their curriculum from a variety of sources.

Your child might need one approach in math and another approach to phonics. In general, no one supplier can provide all you need.

Even when using a variety of suppliers, you will likely need to modify whatever you choose. Let me give you an example. Picture the learning disabled child with an attention problem. His mother sits him at the kitchen table with a worksheet of thirty problems. The page's multicolors, while attractive, are almost overwhelming for this child. The problems are closely spaced with insufficient room to perform calculations because this child's handwriting is quite large. This single page can absolutely paralyze a child!

A better initial choice might be to choose a workbook with less color. You can construct a viewing box out of posterboard, consisting of a small viewing window that is placed over the current problem. This blocks out the other work and allows the child to focus on one problem at a time. Cutting out one row for him to do will reduce the number of problems visible at a time. Numbers that are visually too small can be enlarged with most copiers. Any or all of these modifications can take a workbook for a standard curriculum and transform it into something a challenged child can use successfully.

There are other factors to remember when you choose your materials: your teaching style, your budget, the other children in the family, and the time required to work with the challenged child. As stated before, many parents of challenging children feel that 20 percent of their family receives 80 percent of their energy and attention. Are there modifications you can make to share the teaching time required? In our home we have the older children take turns doing drills and computer work with the younger children. We even use this as an opportunity for them to earn extra money or other privileges.

Be realistic about the time you have available to make or use extraneous materials. It may be your heart's desire to hand-make learning games, charts, and other reinforcing materials, but it might save your sanity to take a trip to the teacher's store to purchase these items.

If challenging children spend all of their time working on problem areas, they will learn to dread schooltime. Our goal should be to create a balance each day of things they feel good about and things they struggle with. In our home, math and phonics are the most tedious and time consuming. Therefore, I make certain that history, geography, science, Bible, and the arts are hands-on, project-oriented, and as much fun as I can squeeze out of them. The children are assured that if they get through the hard stuff, then they will be able to use their considerable strengths in the other subject areas.

How does this work? It is limited only by your imagination. We recently toured through ancient history (again). Though my daughter had considerable difficulty with the minimal assigned reading, she loved watching a video, building a pyramid, doing pop-up books, working with clay to carve hieroglyphics, and using Sculpy to make tomb artifacts. These activities did not require her to focus on her weakness—reading—but allowed her to experience success. Doing well further encouraged her to read the two readers she was assigned to read independently, and the unit was satisfying and rewarding. She is able to retell volumes of stories about the time period studied—far more than if I had merely required her to read out of a book.

The learning experts refer to this approach as making sure your instruction has a balance of remediation and compensation. *Remediation* means going to the core of the issue and working directly on the weaknesses, and is most appropriate for the younger child or the child with less severe problems. *Compensation* means teaching strategies for dealing with the issues, and is more appropriate for older children or those with severe problems. Keep in mind that the older your student, the more he will need to focus on content areas, like history and science, to prepare him to deal with upper level courses.

For the younger child, if this makes you feel overwhelmed by your teaching and preparation load, focus on the basics and pick fewer skills to work on at a time. Then add in things like science and history, the content area of which will be repeated *multiple* times throughout the school years. Take a look at a sample scope and sequence, such as the one at www.worldbook.com (see parent resource center) and see how many times plants are studied from kindergarten through twelfth grade. The amount of repetition, with ever-increasing complexity, is staggering.

What Are Your Options?

Just as there is no one way to homeschool, there is no one way to homeschool a challenging child. This can be frustrating because as parents, we want an answer! We want to know what to do and how to do it so that our child will learn.

There are a number of ways to arrive at this learning state:

1. Partner with your local public school. Be forewarned that this is a matter of some controversy within the homeschooling community. Those who are deeply concerned about government intrusion into homeschooling will tell you to never set foot near the public school. Yet, where does that leave the parent who truly needs help but cannot afford to secure all services on a private basis? In my own case, we have a beautiful arrangement where we take some special services from the public school and do the rest of the program at home. My daughter's reading specialist and I have formed a respectful partnership. I gain a tremendous benefit from her expertise, and she empowers me to keep my daughter at home to complete her work. Other families I know go to school for speech therapy. To condemn all such arrangements in order to forestall government intervention into the lives of all homeschoolers is shortsighted.

2. Another option is to work with a consultant on a private basis. The Home School Legal Defense Association (HSLDA) offers a special-needs consultant. Almaden Valley Christian School, led by special-needs author and consultant Sharon Hensley, can help you design a complete program. Christian Cottage Schools, with Mike and Terri Spray, are available to help you plan your program. Dr. Joe Sutton of Exceptional Diagnostics offers testing and curriculum consultation. (Contact information for each of these is in the resource section.) Their fees vary greatly, as do the level of services they offer. There are many more consultants available, but these are ones with whom I have had personal contact and experience.

3. You can design your own exclusive program. Become an expert on your child's challenge and design your own therapies and approaches. The limitation to this approach is you will need to give yourself time to educate yourself and get up to speed on your child's limitations and the best practices for dealing with them.

A word needs to be interjected here about costs. School services are free. Private services can be expensive and usually will not be covered by insurance. Insurance will generally cover some portion of therapy expense, like speech therapy or occupational therapy, but will usually not cover educational consultation to develop a homeschooling program. That said, you might have to be creative to find what you need.

Some services may be subject to reimbursement from a Flexible Spending Plan, sometimes called a "cafeteria plan." Under an FSP, you can elect to deposit pre-tax dollars into a special spending plan. Then you pay authorized medical expenses from pre-tax income at considerable savings. Check to see if your employer offers this.

Do you live near a university or medical school? In some university clinics, graduate students learning to be therapists can provide services at great savings.

Finally, there are some home therapies you may discover, such as Straight Talk for speech or Audiblox for learning disabilities. (Some of these are discussed later in the resource section.)

Before You Sign on the Dotted Line

Beware that it is a seller's market. Whether you are looking for curriculum or special therapy programs, look closely before investing your child's future or your money. Anyone can write a program and sell it. Some are good, and some are useless. Here are some tough questions to ask:

• Is this approach/therapy based on scientific research? If so, it was tested on a large sample so results can be generalized to other people. It wasn't used just with the author's three children who did beautifully, so your child will too. It also means the researchers were objective. They weren't affiliated with any company that might benefit from their results. In true scientific research, procedures are compared with a control group, which is a group that did not receive the therapy or program. Finally, the results were measured statistically so the relationships between the numbers can be seen.

• How long has the company or supplier existed? This is not to say that a new, groundbreaking approach doesn't exist, but the longer something has been working, the greater the likelihood it will work.

• Especially if you are expending large sums of cash, is there any guarantee? What are the financial implications or penalties of opting out of the program?

Homeschool IEPs

"What does your child's IEP say?" This is a question you are likely to hear among special-needs circles. It stands for Individualized Education Program and refers to the formal plan a public school is required by law to have once there has been a diagnosis of a disability.

Although an IEP is not usually formally necessary when homeschooling a special-needs child, giving some thought to the components of an IEP can be very helpful, especially when you design your own curriculum. Seeing a written plan and set of goals in place helps keep you on track for the year. It also provides you with documentation of your homeschooling activity in the unlikely event that your homeschooling is called into question.

Your IEP should include the following components:

1. Documentation and comments concerning your child's current ability level. Note how she is doing *now* in the areas of math, reading, and written and oral expression. This can be in the form of formal assessments or samples of her work. (A list of suggested items to include is in chapter 3 under the heading "Take Your Child's Learning 'Pulse.'")

2. Make yearly and short-term goals for each area of weakness. What do you want your child to learn this year or this month?

Make goals short and specific. For example, for the first quarter of the year, your goal might be to recognize the beginning sounds of five consonants: b, c, m, l, and p.

3. Note what materials and methods you will use. List the books, materials, or special services you plan to use.

4. Finally, evaluate how it's going. Once a quarter, evaluate the child's progress toward the short-term goals listed.

How do you determine appropriate goals for your child? There are several publications to assist you:

- *Practical Guide to Writing Goals and Objectives,* by Frances Steenburgen, Academic Therapy Publications, 1981.
- *The IEP Manual,* by Jim and Debby Mills, available from NATHHAN (www.Nathhan.com; 208-267-6246).

How can you tell if your efforts are bearing fruit? Sometimes the progress is big and obvious. Often it is small and incremental. Sharon Hensley from Almaden Valley Christian School puts it this way: "For the majority of families, progress is *not* the big 'send off the fireworks' kind of stuff, but the small, daily-grind type of progress that is often harder to see. I encourage my families to think of progress as small steps forward from wherever their child is now—not as 'how close to normal' are they. I think homeschool families with special-needs kids often feel discouraged and defeated because they don't give themselves credit for the small daily progresses, like a child attending for 10 minutes instead of only 5 minutes, or a student working 10 math problems all in the right direction!"[3]

The Very Young Child

Do you have a very young child whose development you are concerned about? Close consultation with your pediatrician is your first responsibility. Your doctor can compare growth patterns against proven normative charts and tell you appropriate milestones for each age of development. The best thing you can do for younger children (prior to school age) is to get a listing of those developmental milestones and work on those as a goal list with your child in close consultation with your physician. Even if he seems "far behind," just work through the skills in order and honor your child's timetable. These lists of milestones are available everywhere—from your pediatrician for free, but there are also books. One that we used was called *Slow and Steady, Get Me Ready* (Xulon Press, 2003) by June Oberland. It gives day-by-day activities to do with your child from birth to age five.

Joyce Herzog also has written two neat volumes called *Luke's School List* and *Luke's Life List* (www.JoyceHerzog.com). They each list incremental steps of development in academic skills and in life skills. If you are preparing your own program, these books are wonderful!

General Principles of Program Planning

Before we launch into a discussion of specific teaching ideas, there are a few bottom-line priorities you should have settled in your heart before you begin your program:

• It is critical that you decisively answer the question, "Why homeschool?" Your convictions should be firm, and you should be in complete agreement with your spouse. If either of you is against the idea, the stresses left on the other spouse to go it alone will be overwhelming. The Bible says that a house divided cannot stand (see Mark 3:25). The same is true for a homeschool.

• Children must know what is expected of them. Send a clear, positive message that putting forth their best effort is important. Bring them on board as your partners in learning and respect their input, whenever reasonable.

• Remember that repetition and routine create good habits.

• Begin with realistic, bottom-line priorities for your child. It is unrealistic that your child will become fluent in Greek in one semester. It is realistic that he will learn to count from 1 to 25. Write down your goals for the child, being as specific as possible. This is your IEP.

• Don't overreact to your child's difficulties. Children can be tremendously sensitive to your feelings, and such overreaction will only make them feel greater pressure. True, you may be sad and frustrated, but your child is undoubtedly feeling the same emotions. He needs you to be the adult and be in control of your feelings and help him learn to control his.

• Remember to say and think positive things about your child. Talking to others in earshot of your child about his strengths is powerful. A mention to your spouse, such as, "Johnny did an awesome job writing the letter A today," will build his self-esteem and confidence. As a labeled child, he may feel that he is damaged somehow. He must experience success so he can begin to unlearn a failure syndrome. Deborah in California writes this of her challenging child: "She needs to succeed at something desperately, as she feels like she can't do anything."

• We all want our children to have motivation, but remember that intrinsic (self-directed) motivation is usually not learned until extrinsic (motivated by outside circumstances) motivation is mastered. It is more powerful to say to your child, "You may not play until your work is done." Intrinsic may only come later after their character is fully developed and they have matured sufficiently and their goals and passions become the source of motivation.

• Help them to see the relationship between effort and improvement. Prove to them that they *can* learn. By experiencing small successes, they begin to see that there is a correlation between trying hard and being successful.

• Establish control in your house. Life with a challenging child can feel out of control. Make sure your discipline and boundaries are clear and consistent.

• Give children small choices. Would they rather do math or reading first? Would they like the yellow pencil or the green pencil? This helps them to feel a sense of control and will lead to greater cooperation.

• Be sure to relate new information to already known information. When studying fractions, talk about pizza! What is in your environment that they can relate to?

• Abandon the concept of grade level. Your child is at his level, and that's where he is! Organizing children into grade levels is how schools manage large groups of children. You are not a school. You are nurturing your child. Dawna—mom of an autistic, dyslexic child—writes, "Because of my son's delays I have been able to be much more open to going slowly and not feeling like he is behind. This has saved me much heartache and sleepless nights."

• Focus on your goal—a godly, functioning child. If I am responsible for how this child is launched into the world, I would have them be spiritually grounded, wholesome, respectful, and polite rather than a Latin scholar. Michelle, mom of a challenging child, writes: "Engage in daily prayer about what the Lord would have your children learn, and stay focused on the big picture. Don't get bogged down in the day-to-day trials."

• Show children that knowledge has relevance to their lives. Why learn to read? So they can learn God's Word. Why learn math? So they will be paid accurately by their boss and treated fairly in the marketplace.

Joyce Herzog, author of *Learning in Spite of Labels,* gives a terrific reality check for establishing purposes for our child's learning:

Teach reading so the child
Can read the Scriptures by himself.
Teach math so the child
Can take care of his toys and his money.
Teach history to save a child
From repeating someone else's mistakes.
Teach language so the child
Can clearly communicate the truth.
Teach a foreign language in order to
Communicate with a pen pal or missionary.
Teach science so the child can marvel
At God's creativity and power in nature.
Teach safety so the child will be able to protect
Himself and serve others in time of need.
Teach household skills so the child
Will be able to live on his own one day.[4]

Find Their Passion

Because your children may not have traditional experiences of "success," it becomes even more important to help them discern a passion, or call, for their life. Of course this is a spiritual endeavor as we lead them to living a life for the Lord, but it is also a practical one.

Don't focus on what "all the other kids are doing." This is a dangerous practice that will only discourage you and your children. How do we find out what makes their eyes sparkle? Expose them to a variety of experiences to help them find what they love. You may need to look into some activities you might not have considered before, like golf or sculpture or horticulture. Not every kid wants to be a cheerleader or a football player.

What brings them inward joy? Begin to look for unusual classes. Consider volunteering at nonprofit organizations. Take them to shop at small eccentric shops to see what captures their interest.

Rosalie Fink is a researcher whose findings should be encouraging to us. In *Overcoming Dyslexia,* Dr. Sally Shaywitz reports on Ms. Fink's findings:

> Rosalie Fink has studied a very intriguing and accomplished group of dyslexic men and women, highly intelligent individuals who exemplify the paradox of dyslexia. Possessing at the same time a persisting phonologic deficit and extraordinary intellectual accomplishments, the group includes such distinguished scientists as Baruj Benacerraf, chair of comparative pathology at the Harvard Medical School; Ronald Davis, professor of biochemistry at Stanford University Medical School; Florence Haseltine, director of the Center for Population Research at the National Institute for Child Health and Human Development; and Robert Knapp, emeritus director of gynecology and gynecologic oncology at the Brigham and Young Women's Hospital and the Dana-Farber Cancer Institute at the Harvard Medical School. Some of these scientists are authors of highly acclaimed textbooks and scholarly

articles, and their honors include a Nobel Prize and election to the National Academy of Sciences and the Institute of Medicine. These individuals provide a wonderful example of how dyslexic readers, under the right circumstances, can become skilled readers. What seems to distinguish this group is the development of an unusually strong interest in the very narrow area of study, often while still children or adolescents. As Fink describes it, "By focusing on a single domain of knowledge, many of the individuals with dyslexia become virtual little experts about their favorite topic, sometimes beginning at an early age. For some, early reading interests later developed into high-powered careers; for others, early reading interests developed into life-long hobbies."[5]

My own daughter is a wonderful violinist. Other parents of challenging children report tremendous talent in singing, artistic pursuits, and Scripture memory. Does your child show a persistent interest in something wonderful? Do all you can to encourage it. You may be providing a fertile field for greatness.

Specific Learning Areas

What follows are some suggestions for dealing with specific academic areas and issues. While this list is by no means exhaustive, the intent is to give you ideas to try with your challenging learner. Entire books have been written about each of these areas. What follows only scratches the surface of resources and techniques available, but it is enough to help you begin to think about different ways of doing things. Sometimes a simple modification can make the world of difference. At other times, more drastic measures are required.

ATTENTION AND LISTENING

The average adult attention span is six minutes. Some tune out even sooner. Yet we require children to attend for long stretches of time. Even without an official attention disorder, this can be a challenge! With ADD or ADHD, it can seem impossible. The distractions of a normal school setting may cause a sensitive child to be completely overloaded and over-stimulated. As homeschoolers, we have the blessed freedom to arrange our environment to accommodate this challenge.

A reasonable expectation in this area is that a child sit and work for one minute per year of age. Your child may not be there yet. Start with a minute as your goal and work upward. Here are some other techniques to try:

• Do something at the beginning of worktime to get their attention. You might show a picture and tell something interesting about it, or tell a story.

• Break a large task into smaller pieces. Instead of long sessions of math practice problems, break them up into smaller, more frequent sessions.

• Alternate high-interest tasks with those that are less interesting.

• Look for novel ways to accomplish tasks. For example, children do not need to write a traditional book report. They may make a poster or a diorama to show the story line. The old way is not always the best way.

• Let children move around while they work. They might do a few items at their seat, do a few at the dry erase board, and do a few while kneeling at the coffee table. Incorporating movement keeps them attending. Let them physically change positions as much as is practical.

• We have a set of high-quality earphones for my daughter to wear when she is working. They block out the surrounding noise and really help her to concentrate.

• We also have used a tri-fold poster display board (like the ones used for science fairs) to create a study carrel for her. Cutting up a large cardboard box would work just as well. This cuts down on the visual distractions. Short study times in this environment have really helped my daughter's productivity.

• Give children transition time as you go from activity to activity. For example, announce "Five minutes until table time" rather than requiring immediate transition: "Get to the table—*now!*" When children know what is next, you will receive a higher level of cooperation.

• Say the child's name before you give instructions. This is a signal for them to attend. Get direct eye contact with the child before giving instructions. This may sound elementary, but yelling multiple requests across the house to an attention-challenged child is a waste of hot air!

• Give single commands or requests. Children with attention issues can't process multiple simultaneous requests, yet how many times do we find ourselves saying, "Go to your room, make your bed, pick up your clothes, and read your chapter." My daughter would forget what she was doing on the way to her room! Keep it simple and focused.

• Use short, direct sentences. Repeat as necessary. Don't get irritated if they don't get it the first time.

• It is often helpful to have children repeat what you have told them. Ask them, "Please tell me what I just told you to do."

• Use signal words to direct attention. Some preachers say, "Listen!" when a special point is being made. We can do the same. You might choose to say, "This is important," or "I want you to remember this."

• Use visuals whenever you can. Have pictures of the child's morning routine posted in the bathroom. Draw a sequence of pictures to show the steps to take to get ready for school. These are great non-nagging reminders for the forgetful child.

READING

Think for a moment about the complexity of learning to read. Marks on a paper are translated into concepts. There are predictable stages, which must be worked through to get to that level of understanding. They are:

1. *Phonemic awareness and letter recognition:* In this stage, children acquire the ability to recognize the underlying sound structure of words. They begin to see that words are made up of sounds and that letters represent these sounds. A good reading program will begin with a strong focus on phonemic awareness (because children must be able to hear the difference between sounds like "m" and "n") and include instruction on segmenting and blending words into sounds.

2. *Encoding and decoding (phonics, spelling, and word recognition):* In this stage, children learn to match letters with the sounds. Once students can separate words into sounds (have acquired phonemic awareness), the next step is to teach them to match the letters with those sounds. Writing letters to match the sounds is referred to as *encoding* and is the essence of learning to spell. Saying the sounds the letters represent is referred to as *decoding* and is word recognition. Encoding and decoding must be taught together.

3. *Fluency development:* At some point children learn to read words with some level of automaticity without having to sound out each and every single phoneme. Fluency is the automatic and quick recognition of words without having to sound them out. Many students struggle with this and do not automatically recognize words. This causes a loss in comprehension because so much time is spent in decoding that the child loses the point of the text.

4. *Vocabulary development:* Good reading instruction must include vocabulary development. New words should be defined and linked to something the student already knows so the new word can become part of the child's permanent memory.

5. *Comprehension:* This involves understanding what is read. Comprehension instruction must occur in all reading instruction. Students with difficulty in this area are often unable to sequence events in order, summarize a story, draw conclusions from material, or state the main idea in a passage.

Phonemic Awareness

• As your child learns letters and sounds, play word games whenever the opportunity arises. Ask, "What letter does *bat* start with?" When the child is able to answer these questions easily, stretch them by asking, "Change the 'b' in *bat* to 'c' and tell me the new word." Gaining a facility with sounds in this way will really help your child learn to read.

• Get little fingers involved. Fill a shallow box or pan with sand and let children trace letters (and later words) in the sand as they are learning the sounds. Some parents cut letters out of sandpaper and allow children to feel the shapes as they learn the sounds. Let them practice air writing, in which they use large arm movements to trace the letters in the air. At the very least, let them trace the words on a large surface, like a blackboard. We sometimes trace the letters on our child's back to see if she can recognize how the letter "feels." The more senses involved, the deeper the learning.

• A dry erase board is essential. Your child will enjoy writing on the board, and a smaller one is handy for you to use sitting side by side.

• Let children listen to story tapes and read along. Encourage them to follow along with the text with their finger.

• Plastic letters on the refrigerator or on a baking tray are a cheap, powerful investment. As children learn words, have them make the words with the letters instead of merely copying them on paper. This can also be used for spelling tests as children get older.

• Make a reading guide. Some children need to see one word isolated at a time. Cut a small rectangle out of a bookmark-sized piece of cardboard. When your child reads, expose one word at a time in this reading window. Our favorite reading guide was a small ruler-sized guide with yellow cellophane across the top. It allowed Grace to view one line at a time and the line was highlighted. It helped her focus tremendously.

• As your child learns words, write them out on index cards to build up a word bank. Flip through them frequently. If he seems bored, have him read one word for each lap he runs around the house, or read them while hopping on one foot or on a trampoline. When he has learned several words, lay them in front of him and call out each word. Have him pick up the correct card from the array until all the cards are gone.

• A child with auditory weakness may need more than phonics. They may need a greater emphasis on sight words and the memorization of word families.

*Audio Memory publishes tapes of songs
to learn facts. Kits are available for
math, geography, and more.
1-800-365-SING*

Comprehension Strategies

- Let the child listen to story tapes and retell the story to you.
- Introduce new vocabulary to your child before they read a passage on their own.
- As early as possible, teach your child to highlight, underline, and outline. These strategies help memory but also allow the student to see the logic and flow of a passage, which increases comprehension.
- Talk, talk, talk. Any time your child reads something new or learns something new, have them talk to you about it. Ask questions to check comprehension.

Encouraging Reading

- Have your child make his or her own special bookmark.
- Draw some type of "path" to mark the number of books read. It might be stairs on a ladder or leaves on a tree. Or write out a three-by-five-inch card for each book read, including a brief summary and a statement about why they liked or disliked the book.
- Write personal notes of encouragement to your children. Their curiosity to decipher what the note says is very motivating.
- Get a pen pal. This type of communication can be very motivating for a child.
- Listen to your child read aloud daily.
- Read aloud as a family as often as possible.
- Have your child listen to books on tape while reading along in the text.

MATH

Teaching math needs to be systematic, in small bites (incremental), step-by-step, and relevant. There are two aspects to math: calculation and reasoning. A child may have difficulty with one, or the other, or both. A child experiencing difficulty with calculation will have trouble memorizing facts and computing math problems. A problem with reasoning will manifest itself in difficulty solving word problems and grasping concepts such as fractions, telling time, and counting money.

Math Calculation

• Use manipulatives! Have a good supply of blocks, beans, beads, and sticks to count, add, and subtract. Manipulatives are also available to illustrate fractions and even algebra concepts.

• If your child has auditory strengths, use auditory tapes (such as those available from Audio Memory) of math facts put to music. Say the math facts aloud whenever possible.

• Highlight math facts to be memorized, or write them in red.

• Try to not require excessive copying from a blackboard. Use worksheets or consumable workbooks.

• Use graph paper to help your child keep their columns of numbers in a straight line. This can prevent careless errors.

• Highlight or circle the computation sign and the instructions.

• Reduce the number of problems required. Avoid cluttered pages. Fold worksheets in half so students are not overwhelmed with the number of problems. Require only even or odd problems. Use a photocopier to enlarge worksheets.

• Let your child use rubber stamps or plastic letters to give their answers.

Math Reasoning

• A child confronted with a mass of words and told to solve a math problem will have a difficult time. Spend plenty of time talking about operations and the various words used to describe them. An addition problem might mention words like *total, altogether,* or *in all.* A subtraction problem would have words like *difference, fewer than, how many less than,* or *have left.* A multiplication problem might have words like *product, altogether,* or *times.* For division, look for words like *half of, equal groups, each, separate into,* or *put into groups.*

• Once children know the computation symbols, teach them to break the problem into steps. They even may draw a diagram or chart to solve the problem.

• Manipulatives, manipulatives, manipulatives! Use items around the house for younger children. For older ones, it is worth it to invest in place-value blocks, rods, play money, and scales.

HANDWRITING

Should you teach Palmer, Italic, or D'Nealian? There are choices! The Palmer method is the way most of us older folks were taught. The printing is very ball- and stick-like and the cursive is somewhat fancy. The Italic method, such as the Getty/Dubay Italic Series that is so popular among homeschoolers, supposedly allows the child to transition more easily from printing to cursive. The popular D'Nealian is a mixture of italic and cursive and is taught in many schools today.

Which should you pick? Go to a homeschool supply store and take a look at the options. Try the one that looks the most workable. Then use these tips to make it work.

• A variety of pencil grips are available at teacher stores for the very young child with trouble gripping the pencil.

• If your child has trouble staying within the lines, use a crayon to press hard to make a line at the bottom of the writing line and at the top of the writing line. Your child will *feel* where the letter should stop.

• Tape a guide strip for letter formation on their desk for ready reference.

• Have students work at a chalkboard for a few minutes a day making five to ten *large* tracings of troublesome letters, like b, d, p, and q.

• Teach them to use their pointer finger to track their place on the paper when they are copying from the board or another book.

• To remind them of the left-to-right direction for writing and reading, place an arrow on their desk indicating the correct direction.

• Use a salt box or tray for letter tracing while learning to write as well.

• Teach them to type as early as possible.

• If they have trouble learning to write manuscript letters, consider teaching cursive first.

SPELLING

Many spelling problems are the result of visual memory or visual discrimination difficulties. The following strategies may be particularly helpful:

• Teach spelling rules and encourage their memorization. Teach the rules at the same time you teach phonics rules.

• Write out the spelling words in large print. Practice spelling them out loud.

• Trace the spelling words in the salt box, in the air, or on their back!

• Keep a writer's spelling dictionary for misspelled words. Your child can consult his or her dictionary independently when writing.

• Teach your older student to use spell-check and the dictionary.

WRITTEN EXPRESSION

Children with challenges in this area will have problems getting their thoughts on paper. They may be perfectly able to express their thoughts in other ways—verbally or by demonstration—but the act of organizing their thoughts to write them down is a problem. Their writing often will show a disregard for punctuation, capitalization, and legibility. It is difficult for them to proofread their own work because they do not see the errors.

• Sometimes it is helpful to have the child first dictate his stories, either to Mom or into a tape recorder. An older child can then go back and transcribe the writing from the tape recording. A younger child can have the parent type out the story. Use these strategies to get children excited about writing, while working on their ability to get thoughts on paper by themselves.

• Use wide-lined paper and tell your child to skip lines when writing. This gives room for you to teach him how to do corrections. Circle errors and have the child tell you what is wrong with the sentence.

• Give your developing writer a checklist to check his own work. Items on the checklist include things such as: Is my first sentence indented? Do all sentences end with some punctuation? Does each sentence express a complete thought?

• Give him a homemade dictionary of his frequently misspelled words.

• For writing assignments, choose topics that they *care* about.

• Encourage children to keep a journal and write something every day.

• Find places your child can write to receive free items. Do an Internet search for free educational items. Have your child write and address the letters asking for the free items.

• Teach typing as soon as it is practical.

• Write thank-you notes.

• Practice, practice, practice. This is the only way they will improve.

Kym, mom of eight, writes, "Since writing is almost painful for him, we let him answer questions and do much of his writing on the computer. We remember the goal—to have him write a story, rather than to have him write it by hand."

TEST TAKING

• There is more than one way to take a test. Many tests can be given orally. We have given spelling tests orally while bouncing on our trampoline. We have tested history concepts orally while driving in the car. Do they know the material? That's what matters.

• You also might allow your child to dictate answers to you. The young child might take a spelling test by spelling the letters with plastic letters.

• Don't put time limits on testing.

• Use multiple choice or true/false formats where possible. Supply word banks for fill-in-the-blank questions.

For students with demonstrated learning disabilities, (such as those documented by a public school or private educational psychologist) tests such as the ACT or SAT may be taken untimed and with other accommodations. Contact the providers of the testing to make these arrangements well in advance of the test date.

ORGANIZATION/STUDY/TIME-MANAGEMENT SKILLS

In my busy household, my "hobby" is keeping things organized. With so much going on, if I don't spent some time and effort keeping myself organized and working with each child to get them organized, life would be chaos. All children, not just challenging children, need some sense of organization and regularity. For the challenging child, it is essential. Here are some ideas to get you both organized:

• Have a master notebook or file for each child. It should consist of an area for working papers and a reserve file for completed work.

• A general prescription for organization is to have a place for everything and label as needed. Organize your child's work area, play area, and sleeping area as much as possible to help her focus on the task at hand.

• Provide a daily schedule and stick to it as much as possible. Make sure the child is aware of interruptions to the schedule, such as doctor visits.

• Make children understand an assignment before leaving them to do independent work. Have them repeat the instructions back to you.

• If children are old enough, give them a daily assignment or task sheet. We like to keep ours on a clipboard. They can cross items off as they are completed, and I have an easy way to check their progress. (Of course, you should check the actual work as well.)

• Make use of a kitchen timer. Our brains remember the beginnings and endings of our study sessions. It makes sense to study in short bursts of fifteen to twenty minutes, which allows for frequent breaks that can refresh the mind and actually make the studying process more efficient.

• Have your child alternate the subjects to be studied. Do history reading for ten minutes, then work on an English writing assignment, then do math problems for ten minutes—then begin the cycle over again. This works great for children who have trouble sticking with one subject for a long period of time.

• If an assignment is big, such as a long science chapter to read or a several-page paper to write, help the child learn to break it down into smaller segments. For example, reading five pages a day adds up to twenty-five over the course of a week. Breaking down the work involved in writing a paper means investing a little time into it each day, rather then cramming all the work into one evening.

• Especially for older children, ask them to chart their time for a few weeks to see how the hours are actually spent. If they complain that they don't have enough time to do homework, this method will usually uncover several hours of the day that could be put to better use. Make several copies of the following chart, and over the course of two weeks help your child to analyze how his time is spent.

	MONDAY	TUESDAY	WEDNESDAY	THURSDAY	FRIDAY	SATURDAY	SUNDAY
6:00							
7:00							
8:00							
9:00							
10:00							
11:00							
12:00							

1:00

2:00

3:00

4:00

5:00

6:00

7:00

8:00

9:00

10:00

Sit down with your child and look at how they spend their time.

• Are there short gaps of time that can be used for study bursts?

• If your child has doctor or therapy appointments scheduled, have him pack a study bag to take along so he can work while waiting.

• Help your child to honestly account for the hours or half-hours spent watching television, playing games, on the computer, or on the telephone.

• Investigate studying at different times. There is no homeschooling edict proclaiming that all work must be completed by three o'clock in the afternoon.

• As children attain school age, get them an alarm clock of their very own. If they have a hard time getting up in the morning, their battle is with the alarm clock, not Mom or Dad. Make sure they know how to operate it and set it, then leave them to exercise this responsibility on their own.

Social Skills for Challenging Children

While we have never been asked to leave a co-op group, I am certain we have come dangerously close. My son has bitten younger children. Each of the other children has gotten into spats and personality clashes. This causes problems for them in finding friends, but also for you in finding social support.

Children may have a difficult time socially because sometimes their responses are inappropriate. Clara in Miami has a son with speech/

language delays, ADHD, and idiosyncratic behaviors. She writes of her struggles: "Now that he is older, I'm dealing with how the neighborhood children see him and how that affects his siblings. Since he likes to pace and visualize, it makes other children uncomfortable, so I try to have him not do that in general. I tell him, if you are outside, you must play with toys—no daydreaming! Besides that, his interests are rather different from other boys his age, and he isn't too adaptable. He wants to play dinosaurs, or have a Ben Hur chariot race, or act out history. At first his siblings would come and say, 'Mom, why is N so different. Everybody says he's weird.' I would tell them he is a different learner. He is your brother. Never join in any mockery of him."

As a parent, you may have difficulty in a typical support-group setting. Many of the "perfect families" may have trouble accepting you and your child, blaming your child's behavior on your failure to train. With the tendency of some Christian homeschoolers to be judgmental, it may be a painful experience for you.

It is hard to find like-minded, sympathetic friends. Consider yourself fortunate if you have a special friend or two who understand you. You may have to start your own group, which I have seen done successfully a few times in my area. Do an Internet search for special-needs homeschooling, and you will be astounded at the number of fellow travelers you will find.

As for your children, make some time to practice social skills with them. Talk about how to behave at the dinner table or when company is visiting. Make a game out of the training so they will not feel condemnation for their lack of social skills. One of my earlier books is called *Life Skills for Kids* (Shaw, 2000), and I spend an entire section talking about how to teach manners and how to help your child foster friendships.

Let's look in detail at a social skill that all children need to cultivate: being a good listener. How do you teach your child to be a good listener? One good way is to ask them what that skill looks like and what it sounds like. Take a piece of paper or a small posterboard for each social skill you wish to teach. Make two columns with the headings "Looks like" and "Sounds like." Engage your child in discussion. Ask, "What does being a

good listener look like?" Their response might be, "The person is looking
at you." Then ask, "What does being a good listener sound like?" Their
response might be, "It sounds like silence because they are listening!"
Record their responses on a chart, such as the one below.

Good Listening

LOOKS LIKE	SOUNDS LIKE
You face the person	You are silent when listening
You maintain eye contact	You use a normal tone of voice
You don't make faces	You acknowledge what they say
You sit up straight	You ask for more information, if needed

After the child has brainstormed with you about this skill, look for him
to practice it. Reinforce and encourage him when he does so.

Other social skills you might want to target are: having a conversation,
playing nicely with a playmate, or solving a problem with another person.

Think of this as on-the-ground flight training. A pilot spends a tremendous amount of time in a simulator before he takes the controls of
an airplane that costs millions of dollars. Too much is at stake. The social
situations your child may find himself in are just as risky. Don't send him
in without some on-the-ground practice.

This social role playing is valuable not only for teaching appropriate
behavior but also for teaching healthy responses to challenging situations.
For example, with a younger child, you might practice what to do if a
playmate wants to play something different from what your child wants.
How will he resolve the conflict?

Your older children, no matter how sheltered, will be faced with
challenges in the world. Role-play with them so they will be prepared.
How will they handle the unwanted interest of someone of the opposite
sex, for example? My daughters are quite lovely and have had to learn
how to deal with unwanted advances. Even in the most straight-laced
communities, children sometimes find themselves in unpredictable situations, such as a party where alcohol suddenly appears or where smoking

cigarettes is practiced and encouraged. Give your child tools to deal gracefully and decisively with these encounters and you will give them greater confidence as they explore the world outside of your home. We do not want to think that temptations such as these will be faced by our children, but to fail to contemplate and prepare for them is negligent. This is not the world of twenty, thirty, or forty years ago.

Career Exploration

At about middle school age, your child might want to begin thinking about careers. Make it a family project to research one career a month, either by reading a book or interviewing someone in that job. If asked, many professionals will allow children to work alongside them for a period of time to get a feel for their work.

The *Occupational Outlook Handbook* (OOH) published yearly by the U.S. Department of Labor provides detailed descriptions of several hundred common occupations. It can be accessed free on the Internet at http://stats.bls.gov/ocohome.htm or may be viewed at your public library.

The *Dictionary of Occupational Titles* (DOT) contains detailed information about specific occupations, such as skills required, knowledge and education needed, job responsibilities, work activities, average pay, etc. It can be accessed free on the Internet at http://www.doleta.gov/progams/onet/ or viewed at your public library.

If your child's learning issues stand in the way of college, it is not the end of the world. How do you define success for that child? In our home, we don't care if our children choose to be street sweepers, so long as they do their work to the glory of God, as we all are instructed to do in Colossians 3:23: "Whatever you do, work at it with all your heart, as working for the Lord, not for men." Someday our children will leave our home, and we want to have examined all the occupational options available for them.

A valuable exercise for your junior high and older child is to choose five jobs of potential interest. For each job, research the following questions. Assemble your answers into a career exploration notebook.

1. What is the job description? What does this person do all day? What skills do they use? What is their work environment?

2. What education or training is required for this job? How long will training take and what will be its cost?

3. What are the pay and benefits of this job?

4. What are the advantages and disadvantages of this job?

Spend some time thinking about their findings. Use this as a springboard for them to pray to God about what their future holds. Ultimately, they are in his hands. Our job is to equip them to fly.

CHAPTER TEN

Getting Help

Finding Professionals and Resources

*Even if you are on the right track, you'll get run
over if you just sit there.*

—Will Rogers

The number of options to help in homeschooling children with special needs is growing. Publishers and curriculum suppliers are hon-
oring the marketing adage that you find a niche and fill it. But as parents
of children who use these products and services, we must be wise con-
sumers. There are proven and unproven strategies for dealing with ADD,
learning disabilities, physical issues, etc. A glance at your Internet news
supplier's ads will reveal any number of businesses willing to help you
solve all of life's problems.

On the other hand, many parents have found solutions to long-
standing problems through approaches like modifying the diet, biofeed-
back, brain reprogramming exercises, and the like. Don't be hasty in
choosing an approach, but don't be hasty in discarding one either. Do

your homework, pray for guidance, and proceed.

While one-on-one learning is the tremendous benefit of homeschooling a child with a challenge, don't think that you have to do everything alone. There are resources and programs to increase the effectiveness of your instruction.

For example, consider the effectiveness of an approach combining diet, behavior modification, and specialized teaching techniques. Its potential is much greater than a single approach alone. On the other hand, if you try a variety of things at the same time, you may have trouble sorting out what is actually working! A balanced approach might be to make changes one at a time so you can evaluate the effectiveness of each.

Know Your Child

Your first challenge, as stated early on, is to do your homework. Become an expert on *your* child. Observe him in a variety of settings and take notes on his behavior and reactions. If you suspect a certain disability or difference, or you feel that your child has a different learning style or personality style than yours, don't stop with just the information in this book. Read, read, read—and then read some more. Learn as much about your particular issue as you can. This knowledge is power.

Mary H. in Texas faces physical and behavioral challenges with her son. She writes: "If the parents are Christians, pray about it. Get lots of information about your child's problem so that you will know what to ask the specialist, and what to expect from them as well." If you have done your homework and then choose to pursue a professional evaluation, you will not need to spend more time becoming educated. You will know what questions to ask and will be able to focus your time on learning how to help your child, rather than on educating yourself.

If you suspect a reading disability, I strongly caution you: *Don't wait.* There is a great deal of difference between a late bloomer and a child with a disability. If your child is simply maturing slowly and you are not particularly concerned about his cognitive development, then a hurried approach is not what is needed. If you suspect a true disability, however, don't wait to confirm or discount your suspicions. The research in this area clearly confirms that the earlier the problem is dealt with, the greater success the child will experience.

Schwab Learning, a premier source for information on learning issues, says: "The three key research conclusions that support seeking help early are: (1) 90 percent of children with reading difficulties will achieve grade level if they receive help by the first grade; (2) 75 percent of children whose help is delayed to age nine or later continue to struggle throughout their school careers; (3) if help is given in fourth grade, rather than in late kindergarten, it takes four times as long to improve the same skills by the same amount. People who understand these research conclusions realize they cannot afford to waste valuable time trying to figure out if there really is a problem or waiting for the problem to cure itself."[1]

Wishful thinking won't make a child better.

You also may need to be persistent in your search for help, especially if you are seeking help from government–funded sources. In the area of learning disabilities, many school districts will not even admit a child for evaluation until that child is functioning two years below grade level. Other special service providers, such as speech therapists or occupational therapists, have a staggering caseload and may be difficult to convince that your child deserves services. Mary H. reminds us: "I have also learned that at times, I have to 'fight' with professionals to get services that my son may need. But he's worth it!"

How to Find Professionals

If you have chosen to get a professional diagnosis, what should you do next?

Start with your family physician or pediatrician. Let him rule out any organic reasons for your difficulties. He also can be a good source for referrals to other professionals.

Michelle in Wisconsin counsels: "If I were going to seek outside help, I would first go to my pastor or other church elders/leaders. They can probably direct you to someone with experience and/or biblical advice that would be more solid (and cheaper!) than other sources."

If you are near a university, especially one with a speech pathology department, it can be a source for information and referrals. A university teaching hospital often has clinical services available for a reduced fee as well.

Kym, mom of eight, writes, "Ask around for word-of-mouth recommendations before going to a professional. Make sure your personalities work together, since you will be working together for a long time."

You also might use the Internet. This is a great tool for researching your specific issues because it will allow you to gather a great deal of information quickly. (In the resource section of this book, several key Web sites are referenced to get you started.)

If you choose to work with more than one professional, make sure they all are communicating with one another. What is needed is a team-work approach, with the parents as coaches.

Carrie in Arizona advises: "Pray for a godly, caring person to handle your evaluation. Pray, pray, fast, fast some more, and pray. The Lord is big enough to take all of your stress, anxiety, and emotions off of your shoulders, but you have to hand them over. Your main goals when walking into your evaluation are getting help for your child and insisting that *you* know how to help your child." In the end, we parents will be doing much of the work at home. Pray for wisdom early on and continually.

First Things First

Let's say you are dealing with more than one issue. Perhaps you have a personality clash with your child, your methods of discipline are not bearing fruit, and you have some concern for your child's academic ability. What do you tackle first?

Work on those everyday things that drive you crazy, like self-care and family routines. Allow yourself and your child to experience some success in these areas and then branch out into other areas.

Give your new program or approach sufficient time to achieve results. New routines take about a month to become truly internalized. If, for example, you have decided to implement a token program, don't give up if your children aren't completely on board in the first two days. Your consistency and commitment will make or break the program.

Seeking a Public School Evaluation

If you have decided to approach your public school to obtain a learning disability evaluation, how do you find out if your child is eligible for special education? Rather than a casual phone call, I suggest you send a written request to the director of special education or the principal of your child's school. In your letter, express your concern that you think your child has a disability and needs special education help. Ask the school to evaluate your child as soon as it is practical.

They may agree to an evaluation, and they might not. If they agree, then the school must evaluate your child at no cost to you within sixty days of their consent. But be advised that the school does not have to evaluate your child just because you have asked. If the school refuses to evaluate your child, they must let you know this decision in writing along with the reasons for their refusal. Along with their communications with you, they should have furnished to you a document that delineates your rights to an appeal of their decision. If you choose to challenge their decision, you follow the procedure prescribed in that literature.

Pick Your Professional

Who can diagnose whether your child has a learning disability or ADHD? The answer is not that simple.

If the issue is raised by a teacher or parent, a school staff member, or a judicial officer, your local school district must perform an educational assessment. As noted above, if you are the first person raising the issue, the school has the discretion to deny an evaluation. Keep in mind that this school district evaluation is to diagnose learning disabilities. They cannot diagnose ADHD, but they are your partners in gathering information for the diagnosis by another professional.

While a plethora of professionals may suggest the presence of ADHD, only a clinical psychologist, a neuropsychologist, or a psychiatrist may diagnose ADHD. If the diagnosis is made by a nonmedical person, you still need to go to your family doctor to get a prescription. Usually a parent will get an assessment from a Ph.D., then take it to the family doctor, who then will prescribe and monitor the medication. If your diagnosis is made by a psychiatrist, this medical doctor who can prescribe medication.

On the other hand, that same psychiatrist or medical doctor cannot make a diagnosis of a learning disability. The LD must be diagnosed by a clinical psychologist, school psychologist, educational psychologist, or neuropsychologist.

A school counselor, social worker, or other unspecified "educational specialist" cannot diagnose either of these conditions, although these individuals may be involved in your treatment program.

If you are pursuing these evaluations on a private basis, there are several questions you should ask:

- What is your license or certification?
- What are your areas of expertise?
- Do you specialize in treating a particular age range of patients?
- What are your fees? Hourly rate?
- How many hours will the assessment take?
- Do you accept insurance? How is it billed?
- Will you communicate with the school or with other professionals? What are the additional fees for any consultation?

You want to work with professionals who will respect your input as a highly-involved homeschooling parent. Clara in Miami is a registered nurse, currently a stay-at-home mom. Her son has speech/language issues as well as behavioral concerns. She is having a hard time finding professionals to help her. She writes: "I am still looking for somebody who would work with me in a peer relationship. Because I am the mom, they should anyhow, but at least in their eyes they should because I am a nurse.

I am looking for somebody I can explain our issues and concerns to who would work alongside and provide insight and guidance. Unfortunately, at least where I live, this is hard to come by, if it exists at all. The mentality that 'I am the professional and I know what's best' is firmly ingrained among health professionals here. They are not at all used to moms being aggressively aware, active, and involved in their children's education."

A private evaluation can be quite costly. In our situation, we used the public school for our daughter's learning disability diagnosis but consulted a private psychologist to diagnose her ADD. The private psychologist gave his findings to our family physician, who actually prescribed the medication. That private evaluation cost around two thousand dollars.

The question arises: How do you pay for these services? Private insurance may cover a portion of the psychologist's fees. You might negotiate to pay the fee in installments or ask for contributions from relatives.

Still wondering about seeking professional help? There can be considerable obstacles along the way. K in Illinois, whose daughter suffers from bipolar disorder, writes: "Do it! When in doubt, find out. Knowing what we've been struggling with over the years has helped us to realize we weren't just 'bad parents' because our daughter behaves the way she does. It has also enabled us to face her disorder in a fully informed way and to begin treatment."

The Assessment Process

For a learning disability, the assessment involves several components:
- an assessment of intellectual potential (or IQ), such as the Stanford-Binet Intelligence Scale or the Woodcock-Johnson Pyscho-Educational Battery
- an assessment of the child's information-processing or motor ability (to isolate whether the learning difficulty is in the visual, auditory, or motor system)
- an assessment of current educational achievement (grade level), such as the Wechsler Individual Achievement Test or the Wide Range Achievement Test

An evaluation for ADHD usually involves:

- an extensive developmental history
- detailed questionnaires to the student (if older), his parents, and his teachers. One of the most common tests is called the Conners' Parent Rating Scale, developed by C. Keith Conners, Ph.D. It asks the evaluator to look at eighty categories of behavior and rate whether the behavior is "never present," "seldom present," "often present," or "very often present."
- other tests at the discretion of the psychologist. Some use a computer-based program that measures a child's ability to attend or their tendency to act impulsively. This is not yet standard practice, and your professional may or may not offer this assessment.

We prepared our daughter for the testing experience by telling her she was going to go play some games with some nice people. Although she is a bit shy, she adapted to the situation very well. We did not tell her too far in advance because she would have fretted for an unnecessarily long time. We told her just beforehand and answered all her questions about the process.

If you choose to have your child evaluated by the school district, the following is an indispensable book, full of sample letters, checklists, and more: *The Parents' Complete Special Education Guide* by Roger Pierangelo, Ph.D. and Robert Jacoby (West Nyack, N.Y.: The Center for Applied Research in Education, 1996).

There is no magic pill or easy-to-do formula that will solve all your child's problems. There is no one program that will answer all your questions and concerns. Digging for the causes is hard work. Doing the work needed to help your child is even harder.

Other Professionals

Other types of specialists you may need to consult to help you sort out your child's difficulty may be:

- Allergist/Immunologist: Food and environmental allergies can cause learning and behavioral problems.

- Educational Advocates: There are attorneys who specialize in education issues.
- ENT (ear, nose, and throat specialists): If you suspect a physical cause for hearing or speech problems.
- Neurologist: Can assess for physical reasons for problems.
- Neuropsychologist: A licensed clinical psychologist who works with learning and behavior.
- Nutritionist: Can help sort out food allergies or sensitivities.
- Ophthalmologist: Medical doctor specializing in the eyes.
- Developmental Optometrist: Specializes in muscular problems with eyes and tracking issues.
- Functional Optometrist: Can spot visual differences that can interfere with learning.
- Pediatrician: Your first stop for a physical exam and referrals.
- Physical/Occupational Therapist: To work with motor problems.
- Psychiatrist: For medications and behavioral issues.
- Psychologist: For ADHD evaluation and counseling.
- Sleep Disorder Specialist: To determine if this is a factor in behavior issues.
- Speech Pathologist: Will assess any problems with speech/language processing and/or expression.

A Final Thought

I have a hard time asking for help. I was raised with the false belief that asking for help was a sign of weakness. Part of my journey has been accepting my weakness and relying more on God's strength. I have changed in the following ways:

• I am now a lot less self-righteous. A few years ago I would have told you that homeschooling held all the answers to all your problems, and I was convinced that I was right. I don't know all the answers for my *own* situation, let alone yours. But I *do* have total confidence in the one who holds the answers to all of life's questions, and I can approach him with confidence, resting in his strength.

• I am a lot more focused. My prayer is that my life with my children has a greater impact because I am not blown to and fro by our circumstances. I accept them, I work with them, and I move forward in life.

• I have a greater appreciation for who God is and how he works through people and circumstances. I don't know why the Lord allows challenging children in our lives, but I do know that he can use them to bring us closer to him. Rather than grumbling to God about your situation, ask how he can use you and your challenge. In the Amplified Bible, Psalm 4:1 says, "You have freed me when I was hemmed in and enlarged me when I was in distress." How will the Lord enlarge you in your distress?

Isaiah 43:19 says: "I am making a way in the desert and streams in the wasteland." God can bring beauty where you see only ashes. Cling to him, rely on him, and watch as he unfolds the plan and the purpose for your challenge.

God bless you!

Notes

INTRODUCTION

1. *Merriam-Webster's Collegiate Dictionary,* s.v. "challenge."

CHAPTER 1

1. Sally Shaywitz, M.D., *Overcoming Dyslexia* (New York: Alfred A. Knopf, 2003), 30–31.

2. Sherry Bushnell and Diane Ryckman, eds., *Christian Homes and Special Kids* (Porthill, Id.: NATHHAN/CHASK, 2003), 4–5.

3. Steven E. Duvall, D. Lawrence Ward, Joseph C. Delquadri, and Charles R. Greenwood, "An Exploratory Study of Home School Instructional Environments and Their Effect on the Basic Skills of Students with Learning Disabilities," *Education and Treatment of Children* 20 (1997): 150–172, http://firstsearch.oclc.org/images/WSPL/wsppdfl/HTML/03477/AI8UR/YSH.htm.

4. Ibid.

5. Ibid.

CHAPTER 2

1. "Learning Disabilities," National Institute of Mental Health, http://www.nimh.nih.gov/publicat/learndis.htm.

CHAPTER 3

1. U.S. Department of Education, *Twenty-second Annual Report to Congress,* 2000.

2. Joan M. Harwell, *The Complete Learning Disabilities Handbook* (Paramus, N.J.: The Center for Applied Research in Education, 2001), 21.

3. American Psychiatric Association, *Diagnostic and Statistical Manual of Mental Disorders,* DSM-IV, 1994.

4. Roger Pierangelo, Ph.D. and Robert Jacoby, *The Parents' Complete Special Education Guide* (West Nyack, N.Y.: Center for Applied Research in Education, 1996), 152–53.

5. Corinne Roth and Lisa Strick, *Learning Disabilities: A to Z* (New York: Smith, The Free Press, 1997), 42–43.

6. Ibid., 50–51.

7. Ibid., 59.

8. Shaywitz, 140.

CHAPTER 4

1. Carol Barnier, *How to Get Your Child Off the Refrigerator and On to Learning* (Lynnwood, Wash.: Emerald Books, 2000), 16.

2. Thomas Armstrong, Ph.D., *The Myth of the A.D.D. Child* (New York: Plume, 1997), 29–30.

3. Dennis Swanberg, Diane Passno, and Dr. Walt Larrimore, *Why A.D.H.D. Doesn't Mean Disaster* (Wheaton, Ill.: Tyndale House Publishers, 2003), 108–109.

4. Israel Wayne, "Inside the Brain of a Hyperactive Homeschooler," www.christianadhd.com/inside.html.

5. Eric Jensen, *Teaching with the Brain in Mind* (Alexandria, Va.: Association for Supervision and Curriculum Development, 1998), 50–51.

6. Ibid., 50.

7. James Reisinger, "Blinks: A Phenomenon of Distractibility in Attention Deficit Disorder," www.christianadhd.com/blinks.html.

8. Swanberg, et al, 61.

9. Zan Tyler, "Education and the Drug Conundrum," www.life way.com.

10. Barnier, 19.

11. Karin A. Blich, "10 ADD/ADHD Myths," www.american baby.com.

12. Swanberg, et al, 102.

CHAPTER 5

1. Tim and Beverly LaHaye, *Spirit-Controlled Temperament* (Wheaton, Ill.: Tyndale, 1967).

2. Beverly LaHaye, *How to Develop Your Child's Temperament* (Irvine, Calif.: Harvest House Publishers, 1977).

3. Ibid., 14.

4. Ibid., 16.

5. Ibid., 21.

6. Ibid., 22.

7. Ibid., 28.

8. William B. Carey, Ph.D., *Understanding Your Child's Temperament* (New York: MacMillan, 1997).

CHAPTER 6

1. Cynthia Tobias, *The Way They Learn* (Colorado Springs, Colo.: Focus on the Family Publishing, 1994).

2. Ibid., 152–53.

3. Ibid., 154.

4. Ibid., 158.

5. Jeff Myers, Ph.D., "Learning Styles: Maximize Your Child's Potential," www.Crosswalk.com.

6. Joyce Herzog, *Learning in Spite of Labels* (Lebanon, Tenn.: Greenleaf Press, 1994), 125.

7. Film: *The Pygmalion Effect: The Power of Expectations* (Carlsbad, Calif.: CRM Learning), www.crmfilms.com.

CHAPTER 7

1. Howard Glasser and Jennifer Easley, *Transforming the Difficult Child: The Nurtured Heart Approach* (Tucson, Ariz.: Howard Glasser, 2002).

2. Ibid., 10.

3. Ibid., 14.

4. Ibid., 28.

5. Ibid., 95.

6. Gary Chapman and Ross Campbell, *The Five Love Languages of Children* (Chicago, Ill.: Moody, 1997), 17.

7. Morris R. Schechtman, *Working Without a Net* (New York: Pocket Books, 1994), 9.

8. Ibid., 13.

9. Ibid., 18.

10. Elizabeth Crary, *Pick Up Your Socks* (Seattle, Wash.: Parenting Press, 1990), 40–42.

CHAPTER 8

1. Slogan from National Public Radio program, "A Prairie Home Companion," host Garrison Keillor.

2. Elizabeth Kübler-Ross, *On Death and Dying* (New York: McMillan, 1969).

3. Christine Field, "Resource Room at *The Old Schoolhouse Magazine*," *The Old Schoolhouse* (Winter 2003): 26.

4. Margo Taylor, "Parenting Children with LD," *Discoveries* (Fall 2001): 14.

5. Diana Johnson, *When Homeschooling Gets Tough!* (Tyler, Tex.: Home-Designed Schooling, 2003), 105.

6. Ibid.

7. Sherry Latson, "Preventing Burnout," www.ldonline.org/ld_indepth/parenting/preventburnout.html.

8. Jane Gambill, "Reaching Out to Families Who Home School Children with Special Needs," (Illinois Christian Home Educators, *The Alliant*, Winter 2003): 20.

9. Swanberg, et al, 84.

CHAPTER 9

1. Herzog, x.

2. Brian D. Ray, Ph.D., *Worldwide Guide to Homeschooling* (Nashville, Tenn.: Broadman & Holman, 2003), 78.

3. Field, 26.

4. Herzog, 78.

5. Shaywitz, 117–18.

CHAPTER 10

1. "A Parent's Guide to Reading Basics: Does My Child Have a Reading Disorder or Developmental Lag?," www.Schwab Learning.org.

Biography

Christine M. Field practiced law for eight years before becoming a full-time mommy. She and her husband live and homeschool their four children in Wheaton, Illinois, where her husband serves as chief of police. Three of their four children are adopted, one through a private adoption and two from Korea. They are also active foster parents.

Christine is the author of several books, including *Coming Home to Raise Your Children* (Fleming Revell, 1995), *Should You Adopt?* (Fleming Revell, 1997), *A Field Guide to Home Schooling* (Fleming Revell, 1998), *Life Skills for Kids* (Harold Shaw/WaterBrook, 2000), and *Help for the Harried Home Schooler* (Shaw/WaterBrook, 2002). She serves as senior correspondent and Resource Room columnist for *The Old Schoolhouse Magazine*. Her work appears regularly at Crosswalk.com, Lifeway.com, *Hearts at Home* magazine, *The Proverbs 31 Homemaker*, and others. Her articles on life skills have appeared in *Focus on the Family* magazine and *Single Parent Family*.

Visit her Web site, The Home Field Advantage, at www.HomeField Advantage.org.

Resources

General Resources

NATHHAN/CHASK
P. O. Box 39
Porthill, ID 83853
208-267-6246
www.chask.org
www.nathhan.com

This is the place to start for any type of learning issues. Their Web site is a virtual education in special needs. They have a newsletter, lending library, and helpful Web forums.

This is also the source for an at-home speech therapy program called *Straight Talk*.

HSLDA
P. O. Box 3000
Purcellville, VA 20134
540-338-5600
www.hslda.org

Contact them to learn the homeschooling law in your state. Ask for their booklet on homeschooling special-needs children.

Program Planning/Testing/Curriculum Consulting

Almaden Valley Christian School

Sharon Hensley, M.A.

6291 Vegas Drive

San Jose, CA 95120

408-997-0290

www.almadenvalleychristianschool.com

Sharon Hensley is the author of *Home Schooling Children with Special Needs*. She provides curriculum development and support to enrolled families.

Do you have a child whom you suspect may have a learning challenge? Or maybe, like one in my own family, you have received an "official diagnosis" of learning disability. Has this revelation left you feeling confused, upset, uncertain, and adrift in your homeschooling journey? Rest assured that there is help available and that you *can* homeschool a special-needs child. Sharon Hensley reminds us that we can turn these challenges into opportunities! I had the chance to review her Special Needs Home School Starter Kit and was incredibly blessed. How I came to learn about Mrs. Hensley was surely God's providence. One week after I learned that one of my precious brood had a learning disability, Gena Suarez (editor of *The Old Schoolhouse Magazine*) asked me if I would like to review these products. I was encouraged, educated, and empowered. Let's start with the book. *Home Schooling Children with Special Needs* teaches us to first distinguish between learning differences and learning difficulties. A kinesthetic learner who is forced to do math worksheets would have a learning mismatch. His learning style does not match how he is being taught. A learning difficulty, on the other hand, is when there is a glitch, to use Sharon's word, in how information is processed in the brain. Glitches can exist in the visual, motor, auditory, or attention systems. Sharon's book thoroughly explains each and also explores other disabilities, gives specific instruction for planning a homeschool program, and offers encouragement for dealing with the many emotional issues involved in raising these children. Mrs. Hensley brings warmth and encouragement to her work, and her knowledge is from her formal education (M.A. in special education) and life experience (homeschooling mom of three children, one with autism). After devouring the book, I listened to her audio tapes, "Understanding and Teaching Struggling Learners." This three-tape set features Mrs. Hensley in a live workshop setting where she explains the approaches to teaching the special child. A balanced approach is one that contains remediation as well as compensation. *Remediation* is working on the skills that are at a deficit. *Compensation* is learning strategies to manage material, such as fewer problems on a page, etc. I particularly enjoyed the questions from the audience in these sessions. Real people posed some real problems to Mrs. Hensley, and she gave concrete, helpful answers. Finally, I watched the video, "Program Planning for Special Needs Students." Using her accompanying *Curriculum Planning Resource Guide,* the video took me, step-by-step, through the process of designing a program and choosing resources to use with my daughter. Almaden Valley Christian School operates an umbrella school program, and Mrs. Hensley offers consultation to homeschooling families. AVCS Books has a complete catalog of curriculum materials and resources.

Christian Cottage Schools
Mike and Terry Spray
3560 West Dawson Road
Sedalia, CO 80135
303-688-6626
info@christiancottage.com
www.christiancottage.com

Teri Spray says, "For the past sixteen years, our mission has been to serve, support, and empower parents as they exercise their God-given right to control and direct their children's education. Our purpose is to help parents to feel successful in their homeschooling experience. Often parents choose to enroll with us under our umbrella school program. Here in Colorado they are legally enrolled in a private school and are no longer under homeschool law regulations. Other parents simply want us to evaluate their child and help them to select appropriate curriculum materials. We are currently working with families from Florida to California, but most of our families are here in Colorado.

"Because we view each child as a unique individual, we begin by testing each child one on one with a nationally standardized achievement battery. The entire process takes less than two hours. Now we can understand the child's learning levels in thirteen areas. The tester has also had the opportunity to watch the child process information, listen to guesses, and simply hold a pencil. As you can see, we learn a lot during these two hours. The parents also complete detailed information for us about their family as well as the child. Our next step is to meet with the parents via phone or face to face for a curriculum design. We painstakingly develop an education program item by item with the parents' input. We will also purchase the materials for the family from more than 110 different suppliers. For enrolling families we include suggestions for daily curriculum assignments as well.

"We like to say that special needs are our specialty! Approximately 75 percent of the children we work with have some sort of specific learning need. We work with almost all special needs including developmental delays. Most of the students we help have a specific learning challenge such as dyslexia, auditory processing problems, etc.

"Everyone tells me my greatest gift is encouragement. I know that it is a gift from God given to me to help others. After the testing, we design prescriptive curriculum programs with the parents, and we tailor the program to be suited exactly to what the child needs. Our goal is for the parent to return to us next year and say, 'We had a great year!' This is our priority, not whether or not the family followed a particular prescription or curriculum program.

"We are available throughout the year for counsel and support. We keep a binder handy for each family so anyone can see in a moment exactly which materials the child is using when a parent calls.

"My best advice is to tell you, 'You can do it!' But you don't have to go it alone. It's OK to get help in the process; you don't have to be a lone ranger simply because you chose to remove or keep your child from the school system. However, it is very important for you as the parents to have the final say and authority over all matters pertaining to your child. God has placed parents as the authority over children, not the government. You as a parent understand the needs of your child better than anyone. No one else on this earth loves and understands your child more than you. God gave you this child for a reason, and he will not leave you or forsake you in the teaching, training, and parenting of your child."

> Joyce Herzog
> 1500 Albany Street
> Schnectady, NY 12304
> 800-745-8212
> www.JoyceHerzog.com

Author of *Scaredy Cat Reading, Learning in Spite of Labels, Choosing and Using Curriculum,* and many more titles. Her Web site has tips and a very active message board. She frequently posts answers to questions on the message board. She also does consultation and helps with curriculum planning.

> Exceptional Diagnostics
> Dr. Joe Sutton
> 220 Douglas Drive
> Simpsonville, SC 29681
> www.edtesting.com
> 864-967-4729
> suttonjp@juno.com

Offers tests that parents can administer, such as ADHD screening, LD screening, and career interest tests, as well as in-depth tests and evaluations performed by Dr. Sutton in his home office or in selected major cities. Dr. Sutton is the author of *Strategies for Struggling Learners* (1997).

Planning Your Own Program

Jerome Rosner, *Helping Children Overcome Learning Difficulties* (New York: Walker Publishing Company, 1993).

If you want to design your own skills training program for a child with visual or auditory processing issues, you must have this book! It contains guidelines for pinpointing areas of weakness, then presents specific exercises to work on them. It's not a quick fix; it's hard work and will involve you wading through some information and organizing your approach, but this book is a wonderful resource.

Special-Needs Publishers

EPS—Educators Publishing Service
P. O. Box 9031
Cambridge, MA 02139-9031
800-225-2665
www.epsbooks.com

You probably recognize this name from the popular Explode the Code series. EPS offers much, much more. Their catalog is packed with materials for reading, writing, handwriting, learning differences, and more. Whatever issue you are facing with your child, there is probably a practical, easy-to-use product offered by this publisher.

LinguiSystems, Inc.
3100 Fourth Avenue
East Moline, IL 61233-9700
800-PRO-IDEA
www.linguisystems.com

This company offers a wide variety of materials, from products obviously oriented to professionals to fun games for phonological awareness. You'll receive an education in special needs just by reading their catalog.

Math

Developmental Mathematics by George Saad, Ph.D.
Mathematics Programs Associates
P. O. Box 118
Halesite, NY 11743

Simple, no glitz incremental learning with a lot of practice. You can use any manipulatives you want to illustrate the concept. Your child can skip the extra drill when the concept is mastered.

FINGER MULTIPLICATION: A NEW APPROACH

Multiteach/Johnco by John Gould
331 Doe Run Circle
Henderson, NV 89012
702-914-4441
www.multiteach.net
bethjohn1@pcisys.net

Your child's fingers—the ultimate manipulative! Mr. Gould initially developed the finger multiplication system to help children learn the 6s, 7s and 8s. He expanded it to include the full table. Why and how does this work? Look at your hands. There is a visual symmetry to them. The hands are mirror images of one another. Imagine numbers on each joint of each hand. The child can visualize this or can actually use a pair of white gloves with the numbers written on each finger. The joints from pointer to pinkey are numbered 1 to 10. The job of the thumb is to count, so it does not get a number. The procedure is hard to explain in words, but I'll try to explain a simple problem, like two times two. Starting with the left hand, the student counts using the thumb and moves from the knuckle labeled one to the knuckle labeled two. Now do the same with the right hand. The student notes that two plus two is four, so the answer is four. The system was derived from an ancient Korean method called Chisanbop. If you have a kinesthetic child who needs to touch and feel and move to learn, definitely check this out. It could be a real breakthrough! But just about any child will respond to this fun, easy-to-learn method.

INTELLITOOLS MATH

Number Concepts 1 with Oshi the Otter
800-899-6687
www.intellitools.com

In this program children in grades K through 2 study number concepts in an ocean environment. Record keeping is simple because students' work is saved in a printable portfolio.

The purpose of this program is to help children learn number sense by giving them experiences in counting, numeration, number relationships, and beginning addition and subtraction. The activities take place on three seashore environments: a beach, a coral reef, and a tide pool.

The program is accessible to children with special needs with special overlays or may be used with standard input devices. It's correlated to math textbooks and meets the standards of the National Council of Teachers of Mathematics (NCTM), so it can be used with any textbook in any setting. Blackline masters are provided to make manipulatives to complement the work.

The accompanying teacher's manual contains many off-computer activities to reinforce and extend the computer work. Other helpful activities are presented, such as keeping a math journal.

So, what does this look like? The first activity is the counting activity that takes place on a beach. Seashore animals scurry in and out of a cave while students count using numbers 1–20. The student is either given a Show Me question or a How Many question. With a Show Me question, a number is displayed and the student is asked to show a corresponding number of sea animals. In a How Many question, a number of sea animals are shown and a student is asked to choose the corresponding number. An Explore Mode is available in which students can continue to work on these concepts in a less structured setting.

The next activity is the Greater Than/Less Than "game," which takes place on a coral reef. Sea animals swim to opposite sides of the reef to give the child an opportunity to practice using the concepts of greater than, less than, and equal to, using numbers 0–20. A Question and Answer Mode and an Explore Mode are also available here.

The Addition and Subtraction activity is set in a tidal pool. Here sea animals are washed in or out with the waves. Students practice adding and subtracting the numbers 0–20. The teacher can set a specified problem range to control the level of challenge. The Question and Answer Mode and the Explore Mode are also available in this setting.

The colorful, fun feel of this program is very appealing. My kids loved moving and counting the sea animals. My beginning student immediately grasped some of the concepts. My struggling learner got some great reinforcement from the activities.

Number Concepts 1 sells for $79.95. Because the concepts are universal, it can be used with any curriculum as a great teaching tool or reinforcer.

Touchmath
Innovative Learning Concepts
6760 Corporate Drive
Colorado Springs, CO 80919-1999
800-888-9191
www.touchmath.com

Sometimes I still find myself touching my pencil to a number when I am doing my everyday math. I never thought of it as an approach to computation! TouchMath is a systematic, multisensory approach to teaching children computation skills based on the following:

Each digit, from 1 through 9, has touchpoints. The student is taught "single-dot" touchpoints for numbers 1 through 5 and "double" touchpoints for 6 through 9. In addition, the students start with the highest number and count forward, using the touchpoints. In subtraction, the student counts backward from the highest number to discover the difference. Make sense? Imagine the power of this method when applied to multiplication! To learn multiplication facts, the student learns to skip-count. So, when the twos are mastered and the student encounters two times four, she counts by two for four counts, while touching the touchpoints on the four. In division, the divisor is skip-counted until something close to the number being divided is reached.

I was so excited to learn about this method and immediately began using it with my learning-disabled daughter. She caught on quickly and now doesn't cry nearly as much as she used to when doing her math problems!

TouchMath involves the major senses—seeing, saying, hearing, and touching. While using TouchMath, students see the numerals, say their names, count their value, and repeat the problem and the answer. It is useful for all ages of students, from age three for early learning to the oldest student for remedial learning.

You can call their toll free number, 800-888-9191, to request a catalog or to request the TouchMath teacher training video. The video walks the viewer through the steps of the basic program and is available free through their loan program. The viewer just needs to pay return postage.

TouchMath is a regular part of our program in our home. My daughter is making good progress in math thanks to this innovative tool.

Reading

Susan L. Hall and Louisa Moats, *Parenting a Struggling Reader* (New York: Broadway Books, 2002). This is a good starting point to diagnosing and finding help for reading difficulties.

www.proactiveparent.com
Wilson Language System
508-865-5699
www.wilsonlanguage.com

The number of phonics programs available is staggering. This one, however, is my personal favorite and the one I use at home. I first learned of the program through my daughter's resource room teacher at our local public school.

Developed by Barbara Wilson, it is based on Orton-Gillingham principles of effective reading instruction. (For more information about this research, see www.ortonacademy.org.) It takes the child through twelve steps of learning language, with the intent of showing the child that there is a reliable system to our language. It begins with beginning sounds and moves to syllables, blending, and syllabication. An innovative technique is used called sound tapping. Students touch their fingers, one at a time, to their thumbs. Each finger represents a letter. They next sweep the thumb over the fingers while blending the sounds together into a word. This gives a tactile component to learning individual sounds and hearing them together in a word. The method also stresses that students learn the six syllable types. This helps them to quickly break unfamiliar words into syllables to read with ease. A great deal of research and testing has gone into this program, attesting to its effectiveness. A new program for beginning readers has been released recently called Fundations. It is a complete, effective program for absolute beginners.

Lexia Learning System
2 Lewis Street
P. O. Box 466
Lincoln, MA 01773
800-435-3942
www.lexialearning.com
info@lexialearning.com

Lexia offers computer programs for early readers (ages 4 to 6), beginning readers (ages 5 to 8) and older readers (ages 9 through adult). The approach of each program is drawn from the Orton-Gillingham system, which has successfully helped struggling readers for more than fifty years. The products focus on phonemic awareness, sound-symbol correspondence, and decoding—skills essential to reading success. In each program, students work independently, listening to verbal instructions and clicking on images with a mouse.

Lexia Early Reading (ages 4 to 6) gives students a wonderful opportunity to master phonological awareness. They are guided in a variety of activities by a cheerful cartoon character named Lexie the Lion. Four activities are available from which to choose. Rhyme Time offers eleven units to increase awareness of the patterns of rhyme in spoken language. At each screen, three pictures are displayed, each representing a word. The computer highlights and names the word and then asks the student to click on the two that rhyme. The 350 words available range in difficulty from one-syllable words to two-syllable words with a suffix.

Sound Match is a game to help increase the ability to identify beginning and ending sounds in words. There are twelve units for a total of 350 words, which range from one-syllable words with three sounds to one-syllable words containing four sounds. In all units, three pictures are displayed with the computer highlighting and naming each. In the first seven units, the student is instructed to click on the word(s) that begin with a certain sound. In units eight through fourteen, the student looks for words that end with a certain sound.

Word Snip is designed to increase the awareness of syllabication. A picture is presented to represent a word. Some balls are displayed beneath the word. The student is asked to drag down one ball for each segment in the word.

Sound Slide shows three pictures representing one word each. The student hears a word with a pause between syllables or sounds. They must then click on the picture that represents the sound. A total of 400 words are available in this presentation.

Lexia Phonics Based Reading (ages 5 to 8) offers three levels of learning activities. In Sort B, D, P, the student sorts letters or letter clusters that include the letters B, D, and P. In Touch and Listen, the student matches spoken words with their corresponding short vowel sound. In Match It, the student matches a word, phrase, or sentence with a picture. In Consonant Castle, the student listens to a short word and clicks on its initial consonant. Each correct response helps to build a castle at the side of the screen. In the Bridge game, the student clicks on the correct short-vowel letter to complete a dictated word.

Level 2 activities begin with the game Change, where the student replaces a letter or cluster of letters to spell a new, dictated word. In Spin It, the student matches words with pictures. In Balloons, the student sorts long and short vowel sounds. In Score, the student clicks on vowel sounds to complete a word with a missing letter. In Word Hunt, the student must click the correct word to fill in a blank in a series of sentences.

Level 3 activities include fun word building activities such as Train, Pirate Ship, Word Stairs, Elevator, and Water Works.

The third product I reviewed was called Lexia Reading S.O.S. (for ages 9 to adult). This program offers five levels of engaging learning activities to strengthen older readers. They range in level of difficulty from identifying short vowels and consonants, to completing sentences, to learning Latin affixes! *The material is presented respectfully and would not be considered babyish by older students.*

Each program offers a record-keeping feature to track progress and generate achievement reports. Everything you need is provided to help your beginning or struggling reader. Best of all, *kids love Lexia!* They can work independently for a short period of time each day and master some basic skills by using this fun program. Based on solid research into why children struggle with reading, these programs can help you clear the reading hurdles in your student's life. We have used these CDs with our beginning reader and our struggling reader, and they have both learned a great deal from them.

Reading Reflex
Read America
P. O. Box 1246
Mount Dora, FL 32756
352-735-9292
www.readamerica.net
e-mail: Rachat@aol.com

Many of us teach our children phonics, which in its simplest terms is the practice of sounding out letters to make sounds. The Phono-Graphix philosophy, upon which Reading Reflex is based, is that print is a visual representation of sounds in words by means of sound pictures. Each sound in a word is represented by a symbol, or sound picture. These sound pictures are of language bits that the child already has! When we teach reading using these sound pictures, we are merely giving a face to the sounds the child already has heard and spoken. *This is the opposite of traditional rule-based phonics, which the authors of this program believe sets the child up for failure.* For example, take the rule, "When two vowels go walking, the first does the talking." This is true only 40 percent of the time and will cause tremendous confusion when the child begins to learn words like *eight, bread,* and *house.*

Instead of memorizing rules that may or may not apply in each case, and learning pictures and sounds and letter names, the student using Reading Reflex initially learns forty-three groups of sounds, or phonemes. The letters are introduced in sets of CVC (consonant-vowel-consonant) words, and careful attention is paid to the pronunciation of letter sounds. This sets the child up to learn the letter sound once and be able to put them together into words. Because the sounds existed in the child's world before the letters, this approach allows him to use what he knows to learn the symbols that represent the sounds. Thus the child is taught that letters do not make sounds, but rather represent sounds. Citing a mountain of research, the authors point to a 33 percent reading failure rate where traditional phonics is used. Whole language programs have a 42 percent reading failure rate. The creators of Reading Reflex claim a *100 percent success rate* in teaching reading to people from age four to adult!

The book presents developmentally sound lessons based on years of research in phonological processing and linguistics. Written by Geoffrey and Carmen McGuinness at the Read America Clinic, the approach was researched by the University of South Florida and published in the *Orton Annals of Dyslexia* in 1996. The McGuinnesses claim that they can teach any child to read with this approach, whether dyslexic, a slow learner, or otherwise learning disabled.

The core of this approach is the book *Reading Reflex* (Simon & Schuster, 1998). The beginning of the book is devoted to explaining how we learn to read. The research and philosophy presented are sound and understandable. The parent is next instructed in how to give a diagnostic test to determine reading level. The remainder of the book gives detailed instructions and illustrations to help teach effective reading strategies. There are exercises, hand-on materials, and games—all included in the body of this inexpensive text.

If you do not wish to cut up your book, you can purchase a Reading Reflex Support Pack. This contains all the manipulatives, worksheets, pre- and post-tests and coded stories to be used with the lessons in the text.

The *Extended Student Manual* is available for use by the student who has completed the basic Reading Reflex system. Using books of the student's own choosing, the child is further instructed in phoneme manipulation.

After completing *Reading Reflex,* you may wish to use the follow-up book, *How to Increase Your Child's Verbal Intelligence* (Yale University Press, 2000) by the McGuinnesses. This book presents some research and theory and then dives right into exercises to stimulate verbal intelligence. The authors deal with comprehension, attention, memory, logical reasoning, and creativity. A *Language Wise Support Manual* is available with worksheets for use along with the text. The exercises deal with topics such as making sequenced or graded determinations, building strategies for finding out what words mean from their context, organizing information into sets, establishing connections between words, and practicing inference skills. All of these techniques are presented as easy-to-do games that can be incorporated easily into a homeschool or after school program.

When you think about developing your child's verbal intelligence, it makes sense that learning language has to do with hearing language. Some children are from socio-economic backgrounds where they are exposed to disparate amounts of verbal language. If a child is not intimate with language, it will be much more difficult to learn to read and comprehend. Still, a child who has had little exposure to language is not destined for failure. By using this method, parents can retrain and teach their children to read and comprehend.

Intellitools
Balanced Literacy
800-899-6687
www.intellitools.com

The debate between phonics and sight-word reading continues. Many reading programs land on one end of the spectrum or the other. Balanced Literacy is well named because it contains aspects of both approaches, leaving the teacher the freedom to tailor it to each student's needs. *A tremendous amount of research went into this package.* It was developed with a grant from the National Institute of Child Health and Human Development at the National Institutes of Health. It meets state standards and was researched and evaluated by teachers nationwide. *Why is this significant?* Though a "theory" about some aspect of learning might be used successfully with one child this does not mean that the approach will work with any other child. Balanced Literacy, however, has been tried and tested with all kinds of learners and all kinds of teachers. It can be used by beginning readers as well as students with physical or cognitive disabilities. The traditional keyboard and mouse can be used, or an alternative keyboard is available for children unable to use a standard keyboard. There is even a feature to control the size of the text!

The materials consist of a CD, a teacher's manual with day-by-day lesson plans and reproducibles, and a set of anchor books—hard copies of the stories on the CD. The theory is that the children first learn Onsets, which are consonants and consonant clusters found at the beginning of single syllable words before the first vowel. They then progress to learning Rimes—clusters of letters that begin with the first vowel and continue to the end of the word in single syllable words—or phonograms, word families, or chunks.

The program consists of guided reading of the anchor books; word study activities, both on the computer as well as with blackline masters included in the teacher's manual; structured writing activities in each unit; and self-selected reading. There are nine units, each based on an animal theme. Each unit consists of sixteen lessons and thus covers first grade reading skills. A record-keeping aspect allows the teacher to track and document each child's progress.

Let's walk through a lesson. Each unit begins with the anchor book. The student can listen to the story being read with the words highlighted. Pages may be repeated. Or the student may read the book himself with the audio portion turned off. Next the student is given the opportunity to explore the story and test his understanding by answering questions and getting immediate feedback. The student can then quit or choose to move on to learn the onset song and related activities. The student is given a screen of twelve pictures and is asked to select the picture that begins with the onset sound. Next comes a Rime activity: a song introduces the Rime, and an activity and review are presented. The remainder of the unit includes a pattern book (giving the child practice in specific language patterns) and writing with words (where students create sentences from a word bank of on-screen words). A culminating activity in each unit is the Decodable Book and Writing lesson. The student practices his new skills using a story with a similar theme to the anchor book. In Decodable Writing, the student chooses correct words to fill in sentences with missing words. When the sentence is completed, it is read aloud to the student. Optional games are provided at the end of each unit—a concentration game, an obstacle game, and crossword puzzle game. Each provides immediate feedback and fun review.

The beauty of this program is that *everything you need is integrated seamlessly into the activities!* The activities are multimodal, and they appeal to all types of learners. The teacher can shift the child's focus to the aspects that will strengthen weaknesses. This product can be used to teach all students in a family, whether beginning or remedial, whatever learning style.

The entire Balanced Literacy package sells for $299. If that seems a bit high, consider the fact that this can be used for multiple children for multiple years! The additional blackline masters in the teacher's manual can be copied over and over again.

Teach Your Children Well
P. O. Box 908
Belleville, ON, Canada K8N 5B6
877-368-1513
www.teachyourchildrenwell.com

This is the book that exploded on the homeschooling scene and got us all interested in Michael Maloney and his methods. Mr. Maloney is a long-time educator who started a series of private learning centers across North America that have had tremendous success teaching all levels and abilities of children. In this book he explains his model, which provides for having Behavioral Objectives/Learning Outcomes, Behavioral

Analysis/Behavior Management, Direct Instruction, Precision Teaching, and Directed and Independent Practice. If you think this all sounds like wonderful theory, the proof is in the application, which leads us to the Teach Your Children Well series.

An instructor's manual, student reader, and student workbook are available for K through 2, 3 through 4, and 5 through 6. The books are organized into daily lessons that incorporate all the well-researched theory of Mr. Maloney's main book. The instructor's manual is scripted and even gives correction procedures if the child responds incorrectly. The technique is completely explained in prefatory material in the instructor's manual. The student workbook includes handwriting practice, reading activities, and things like crosswords and mazes. The student reader has practice stories and places where you can track fluency scores. This is a very easy system to use and has the potential to foster tremendous results in your struggling or beginning reader.

Phonics Intervention
Saxon Publishers
800-284-7019
www.saxonpub.com

Leave it to Saxon to create an effective phonics intervention program for struggling readers from grade four to adult! Specifically designed for older students, the materials are not childish, and the system is easy for the teacher to use.

What are the sound principles on which all Saxon programs are based—from kindergarten phonics to calculus? They are incremental development, continual review, and frequent, cumulative testing. All of these are incorporated in the Phonics Intervention package.

The teacher's manual has lesson plans, assessments, vocabulary tests, speed drills, rule charts, and word lists. The student workbook is both a practice book and a reference book, containing reference lists of all phonics and spelling rules, practice reading paragraphs, worksheets, speed drills, assessments, vocabulary tests, and a glossary. A handy box contains card decks of letters, spelling words, pictures, sight words, and vocabulary words, an audiotape of phonetic sounds, and classroom masters of tests and assessments.

I was thrilled to learn about this program. There are lots of products on the market for younger students who struggle with reading—some good, some mediocre. There is not much for older students. This program is fabulous! It is complete and teacher friendly. Saxon once again has thought of *everything* to help students succeed. I was impressed with the tone and completeness of the teacher's manual. It gets right to the heart of tough areas for readers and has a no-nonsense approach that is respectful and interesting for the older student.

The program was created for Saxon by Lorna Simmons, a classroom and special education teacher. She utilizes the latest research and techniques and provides a consistent program—a critical feature for the type of incremental learning that is the hallmark of all Saxon materials. The program builds on reading and problem-solving skills rather than rote memorization.

Carefully planned and executed to the smallest detail, the record-keeping forms allow you to meticulously track your student's accomplishments and weak areas. The flash card decks even have separate dividers for current items and "retired" items, which are to be periodically reviewed.

Even though the program is complete, it is not overwhelming. It is truly student friendly *and* teacher friendly. It lives up to the standard of excellence that we have come to expect from Saxon.

Pecci Reading Method
Pecci Educational Publishers
440 Davis Court, No. 405
San Francisco, CA 94111-2400
415-391-8579
Pecci@prodigy.nct
www.OnlineReadingTeacher.com
At last! A reading method for every child.
Are you confused by all the different approaches to reading? Do you view each new advertisement for a new and improved phonics program

with a degree of skepticism? Mary Pecci does a masterful job of sorting out the hype and helping us get down to the job of teaching our children how to read.

She gives us a good overview of current reading methods and explains that schoolteachers are not taught one correct way to teach reading. Thus, there is no continuity in reading instruction and our children are the victims of educational experimentation. Ms. Pecci gives us a uniform, yet versatile, approach because her book can be used along with any basal reading series or reading material of your choosing.

The method begins with teaching the prerequisite skills: the alphabet (letter recognition) and the sounds of consonants, digraphs, and vowels. She gives plenty of powerful but simple ways to introduce and reinforce these concepts. The student then moves to a reading series of their choosing (many homeschoolers like the Pathway readers). Using the vocabulary list at the back of the reader, the new words are introduced. In the beginning, the teacher gives the student an oral sentence that ends with the word being introduced. For example, to introduce the vocabulary word *come,* the teacher would say, "When I call you, I want you to _____." The student then sounds and underlines the left-to-right phonics clues in the word that will help him recognize it the next time it is encountered. If a word like *and* is being introduced, the teacher gives an oral sentence using the word, such as "This word is *and,* as in 'I see you and John.'" The student then, as always, sounds and underlines the left-to-right phonics clues in the word.

Students are next introduced to sight families as they are encountered, for example, the word *her.* The student names the family *er* and reads the word. A similar approach is followed for short vowel families. For example, with the word *big,* have the student underline *ig,* sound out the *ig* family and say they word. Multisyllablic words are analyzed with each syllable treated as a separate word. Students are then introduced to long vowel families. Any exceptions are introduced with the "What's the clue?" technique. As the child gains facility and a repertoire of phonetic knowledge, approach each new word with these questions: What is the first vowel? What is the family? What is the word?

With a library card and this book, any child can learn to read—and any parent can facilitate the process. Sometimes we overcomplicate our work as homeschoolers. This method gives a complete, simple, foolproof approach. Everything you need is contained within the covers of the book: directions for making flashcards, games, worksheets, and more!

This method can be used effectively with a beginning reader but can also be used for struggling readers. Following the step-by-step procedures, you can help your child achieve reading success that may have once seemed impossible.

Rocket Phonics
P. O. Box 1411
Vista, CA 92085-1411
888-DrPhonics (888-377-4664)
drphonics@rocketphonics.com
www.rocketphonics.com

Rocket Phonics is an affordable, simple-to-use phonics program that claims to outperform traditional phonics programs three to one. Designed for grades K through 3, it can take a non-reader to the fifth grade reading level. Designed by a physician, the program is easy to learn and easy to teach.

Tested and studied by a UCLA professor, forty-three homeschooled students using the program gained 8.9 months in reading skills in just three months.

The program consists of a teaching manual/textbook with jokes, science facts, and riddles; four games, including bingo chips; more than thirty stories; a Rocket Peeker to help your child focus on one word at a time; Play & Read Cards; a supplement folder containing teaching tips and progress charts; and a 100 percent satisfaction guarantee.

Students begin with exposure to the Rocket Phonics Initial Teaching Alphabet. While the English language has twenty-six letters, the creators of this program have created an Initial Teaching Alphabet (ITA) of thirty-six sounds, using often-seen letter combinations. After reading words in ITA, the student is given the normal spelling and easily makes the transition.

This nonconsumable resource can be used for all the children in your family and provides a nice, no-nonsense approach to teaching reading.

Glavach and Associates
P. O. Box 547
Heraldsburg, CA 95448
707-894-5-47
glavach@netzero.com
www.strugglingreaders.com
Core Reading Program
Latin and Greek Word Roots
Phonics Review 1 & 2
Programmed Spelling Review
Reading the News

Have you tried to teach an older child to read? They quickly tire of reading about S-a-m and his c-a-t. There has to be a way to get these children involved in reading while immersing them in more grown-up content.

Dr. Matt Glavach saw this need and dedicated himself to producing such materials. He has a master's degree in special education and a doctorate in psychology. He is the author or coauthor of more than thirty educational programs, including the highly acclaimed Core Reading System.

To quote Dr. Glavach, "The Core Reading System is based on current brain research in reading. Rather than being remedial, it is an intensive and activity-based program designed to connect students to the school's core curriculum. The twenty-five weekly lessons use a core vocabulary from English, biology, science, and social studies curriculums. Students move step-by-step from two-syllable words to words of five syllables or more through a unique spelling approach and timed readings to develop reading fluency. Each lesson is organized by specific words with consistent ending patterns. Core Reading is organized into twenty-five lessons based on consistent word patterns. Using the word pattern approach assists in spelling and transition to reading longer words. For example, words like *plastic, fantastic, scholastic,* and *nation, station,* and *communication* have rhyming qualities that form natural bridges from shorter to longer words in the patterns. Each lesson packet includes spelling, dictionary study for core vocabulary development, an oral word list, and a timed reading selection focusing on the pattern being studied and tied to an important subject in the core curriculum. Each lesson has a similar structure that allows the student to be self-directed and comfortable with what is coming next."

Although I did not personally review Core Reading, I did look at the others listed above. Phonics Review 1 & 2 are nicely done, with clear, ready-to-use worksheets and an accompanying audiotape. It can also be used as a primary phonics program or as a supplement to more intense training. Students begin with an individual placement test to determine proper placement in the program. The audio portion of the program is self-instructional, with the student following along to complete the worksheets. After the audio portion of the lesson, the words are reviewed, and extended activities are available for the student.

Programmed Spelling Review has a similar format. It is designed for students who need to review basic spelling skills and high frequency writing words. It uses audio lessons and student workbook pages. Each lesson presents a particular spelling pattern and then reinforces it through the exercises. The program offers a pretest to determine placement and twelve audio lessons. It is designed for students who exhibit poor and inconsistent spelling. It is easy to follow and can be a powerful reinforcer for the struggling speller.

Reading the News is an interesting, fun program. It uses Associated Press newspaper articles for starting point reading material for students in middle school through adult. Focusing on newspaper article content rather than boring vocabulary lists, the students begin by following along as an article is read on the audiotape. Activities based on each passage encourage the student to think about questions raised by the piece. Words are previewed before the selection is presented. Then numerous word and comprehension activities are offered based on the passage. I have never seen a program structured like this. It is an engaging, creative way to draw students into reading, comprehension, and spelling.

The last product I reviewed was Latin and Greek Word Roots. This one got completely "Field tested"—I used it to teach seventh and eighth grade students in a co-op in which we were involved. The program was easy to use, and the students enjoyed it. Each week, words are introduced in ABC order. Students make study cards, do worksheets, talk about the derivatives, and use the words in their writing. A quiz is provided to test each week's understanding. Every three weeks, one week is devoted to review, with interesting word searches and other activities provided for study. This program is completely laid out for ease of use and my students really enjoyed it—and learned a lot of new words!

Handwriting

Draw Write Now
by Marie Hablitzel and Kim Stitzer
Barker Creek Publishing
800-692-5833
www.barkercreek.com

Handwriting Without Tears
www.HWTears.com

Therapy Programs

Audiblox
U.S. sales representative: Barb Little
701-260-2777
www.Audiblox2000.com
Can "playing" with colorful blocks help your child overcome learning difficulties? Yes, according to the people at Audiblox, makers of an intriguing system of cognitive exercises to develop foundational learning skills. Students work on patterning with blocks, which helps develop a myriad of foundational skills such as concentration, perception, visual and auditory discrimination, and memory. Other techniques, such as

paper crumpling and beanbag tossing, round out this interesting program. Initially developed as a reading readiness program by Dr. Jan Strydom of South Africa, he later discovered that some of these same techniques were helpful to children with learning disabilities, especially dyslexia, attention deficit disorders, and auditory, visual, or central processing problems. Students may begin the program as early as three and there is no maximum age.

The parent works with the student, ideally, for one hour per day, five days per week. The more time you invest, the greater the results with your student. Barb Little, U.S. sales representative for Audiblox, notes, "Generally it takes about 250 hours on Audiblox to remediate an elementary student who is two years behind. For most students it will take fifty weeks of one hour per day five days per week to achieve the 250 hours. If the program is only done about thirty minutes per day, it could take two years on the program. However, if the student can manage to do more than one hour per day, at least initially, the progress will be faster."

Most of the exercises are done with colored blocks. The parent builds a sequence of blocks that the student must memorize, then rebuild from memory. If it is rebuilt correctly, the parent adds blocks to make a longer sequence. This builds sequencing skills and memorization ability, reinforces the concepts of left to right, and practices patterning. These basic skills are crucial to reading success.

Lindamood-Bell
805-541-3836
www.lblp.com
www.lindamoodbell.com

It took me a long time to get my brain around this teaching/therapy concept. But once I got it, it made so much sense!

This goes beyond the phonics/whole language debate to underlying mental processes. People who have difficulty with language usually have some underlying processing deficits. Although I am not a Ph.D. educator type person, I will attempt to explain these concepts.

One difficulty is that of phonemic awareness, which is the ability to perceive sounds in words. Such a person might look at the word *stream* and read it as *steam*. They may add or omit sounds and not know they are doing it. The other difficulty is trickier and involves concept imagery. This is the ability of the brain to process the whole of language that is read or heard. In a sense, the brain sees the language. When I read a word that represents a concept, I can picture the concept on the blackboard of my mind. A student with concept imagery weakness doesn't imagine the whole or concepts of the language. So they may be able to read something flawlessly (have good phonemic awareness), but cannot grasp or understand what they have read. *It can readily be seen that if a child has this type of imagery weakness, no phonics program, no matter how spiffy, will help them!*

The premise of the Lindamood-Bell programs is that the mind can be taught to perceive sounds and image concepts. As the brain learns to think with sounds and letters, reading and spelling improves, the brain can image language concepts, and reading comprehension and higher-order thinking skills can be developed.

The first book I studied was called *Visualizing and Verbalizing for Language Comprehension and Thinking.* Some introductory material in the book expanded on the idea of imagery, noting that language comprehension is more than recognizing words or vocabulary. Rather, true language comprehension embodies the concept of the German *gestalt*— a complex organized unit or whole that is more than the sum of its parts. The author notes, "In the case of language comprehension disorder, the weakness in creating an imaged gestalt—whole—interferes with the connection to and interpretation of incoming language" (p. 13). By encouraging the student's imagery skills, a sensory link is made between language and thought. The body of this text is devoted to showing you how to work with the student to develop their imagery skills. Sample dialogue is included along with some great tutoring on how to ask questions to get the student thinking and communicating. The first series of exercises deal with picture to picture imaging in which the student is led to give a detailed verbal description of a simple picture. Next, the student learns to visualize and verbalize words, sentences, paragraphs, whole pages, chapters, and lectures. This powerful process results in improvement in reading comprehension, oral language comprehension and expression, written language expression, and critical thinking.

Another book is called *Seeing Stars: Symbol Imagery for Phonemic Awareness, Sight Words, and Spelling.* Again, the premise is that the ability to visualize letters can be stimulated. Why is this important? Reading consists of the complex process of accurate phonetic processing, sightword recognition, contextual clues, and oral vocabulary. The child learns phonemic awareness, which is primary to decoding words, and concept imagery, which is crucial to comprehension. *But phonemic awareness must not be confused with phonics.* Teaching phonics does not ensure phonemic awareness. After a thorough explanation of theory, the book takes the student through a series of exercises in learning to image letters, then syllables, then spelling.

The last item I studied was called *On Cloud Nine: Visualizing and Verbalizing for Math.* It is not surprising that many of the same visualizing concepts apply to the sensory-cognitive connection for math. This program uses visualizing and verbalizing to develop concrete experiences, imagery, and computation. Many students who do this for math also have done visualizing and verbalizing for language. Explicit instructions in the text take the student from imaging numerals, a number line, addition and subtraction fact families, word problems, place value, jumping, carrying and borrowing, multiplication and division, decimals, and fractions.

There are individuals around the country who do this type of work with children. To begin to explore these therapy options, check out the above Web site. Workshops, training videotapes, and CDs are also available for the parent who wishes to learn this method themselves.

NEURODEVELOPMENTAL APPROACH

This is based on the concept that the brain is flexible and can make new neuroconnections. Sometimes these connections need to be reinforced. After an evaluation, a neurodevelopmentalist creates a unique program of activities and exercises for your child to strengthen these neural pathways. Neurodevelopmental therapists work with diagnoses such as learning disabled, dyslexic, distractible, ADD, ADHD, hyperactive, autistic, Down Syndrome, Asperger Syndrome, developmentally delayed, cerebral palsied, brain injured, and others.

See neurodevelopmental therapist Kay Ness at www.icando.org or The International Christian Association of Neorodevelopmentalists (ICAN) at www.ican-do.net.

E.L.I.—Essential Learning Institute
334 Second Street
Catasauqua, PA 18032
800-285-9089
www.idhope.com

Essential Learning Institute provides a computer-based sensory integration training program for children with learning problems. Children are tested for specific areas of weakness and are given neurological exercises, via computer, which interlink the visual, auditory, and motor pathways in the brain. Through these multimodal tasks, the pathways of the brain are strengthened. As the process is repeated, the new skill or knowledge is placed into long-term memory.

The student works on seven computer-based exercises: Share, Echo, Word-match, Clues, Copy-write, Quick-pick, and Quick-talk. A component of the program is a dictation session where the student writes words or phrases from the lesson. The sessions are fast moving and engaging for the student. Ideally, the student works for forty-five minutes to one hour per day, on four consecutive days per week. This should take nine months or a minimum of 130 sessions. Students with learning difficulties—including visual and auditory processing, ADD, ADHD, and dyslexia—get good results with the program.

We are currently using this program with our two youngest students. They enjoy the time spent on task and are making good progress in their reading, and their memory is improving.

Organizations/Support Groups/Web Sites

ALL KINDS OF MINDS

www.allkindsofminds.org

Based on the work of Mel Levine, author of *A Mind at a Time* (New York: Simon & Schuster, 2002).

ATTENTION-DEFICIT DISORDER/HYPERACTIVITY DISORDER

National Attention Deficit Disorder Association

e-mail: mail@add.org

www.add.org

CHADD National Association

Children and Adults with Attention-Deficit/Hyperactivity Disorder

www.chadd.org

Child Development Institute

Provides information on classroom interventions for children with ADD and LD.

www.childdevelopmentinfo.com

ADVOCATES/LEGAL EDUCATION FOR SPECIAL EDUCATION

Council of Parents' Attorneys and Advocates

A nonprofit organization on parent advocates and attorneys.

e-mail: copaa@edlaw.net

www.edlaw.net

Wrightslaw

Information on federal laws and an electronic newsletter, "The Special Ed Advocate."

www.wrightslaw.com

ALLERGIES

Food Allergy Network
800-929-4040
http://foodallergy.org

ASPERGER/AUTISM/PDD

The Asperger Syndrome Education Network
Nonprofit source of information, support, and advocacy for Autism
Spectrum Disorders.
e-mail: info@aspennj.org
www.aspennj.org

Autism Research Institute
Information and referral clearinghouse for parents and professionals.
Also offers a newsletter.
619-563-6840
www.autism.com/ari

Autism Resource Network
Bookstore for educators and parents, with reference books and educational toys as well as a quarterly newsletter.
612-988-0088
www.autismshop.com

Autism Society of America
800-3AUTISM
www.autism-society.org

Center for the Study of Autism
www.Autism.org

Bi-Polar Disorders

Child and Adolescent Bipolar Foundation (CABF)
e-mail: education@bpkids.org
www.bpkids.org

Cerebral Palsy

United Cerebral Palsy
www.ucp.org

Cerebral Palsy Magazine
www.cerebralpalsymagazine.com

Developmental Disabilities/Special Needs

Birth Defect Research for Children
www.birthdefects.org

Developmental Delay Resources
www.devdelay.org

Exceptional Parent magazine
www.eparent.com

National Dissemination Center for Children with Disabilities
www.nichcy.org

National Organization for Rare Diseases
www.rarediseases.org

The Sibling Support Project
www.chmc.org/departmt/sibsupp

Down Syndrome

Down Syndrome Home Pages
www.nas.com/downsyn

National Down Syndrome Congress
800-232-6372
www.ndscenter.org

National Down Syndrome Society
800-221-4602
www.ndss.org

National Association for Down Syndrome
wwwnads.org

Dyslexia

International Dyslexia Association
www.interdys.org

Dyslexia Online
www.dyslexiaonline.com

Dyslexic Parents Resource
www.dyslexia-parent.com

Dyslexia Research Institute
www.dyslexia-add.org

General

Child Development Institute
Includes topics ranging from Language Development, Pervasive
Development Disorder, Parenting, Dyslexia, ADHD, Autism, and LD to
Child/Teen Health.
www.childdevelopmentinfo.com

National Center for Early Development and Learning
www.fpg.unc.edu/~ncedl

HEARING IMPAIRMENT

National Information Center on Deafness
www.gallaudet.edu/~nicd

National Institute on Deafness and Other Communication Disorders
Information Clearinghouse
www.nidcd.nih.gov

LEARNING DISABILITIES

Child Development Institute
Suggested classroom interventions for children with ADD and LD.
www.childdevelopmentinfo.com/l

International Dyslexia Association
www.interdys.org

National Center for Learning Disabilities
www.ncld.org

Schwab Learning
Founded by Charles Schwab who was himself dyslexic.
www.schwablearning.org
Great information for parents, especially those who are new to dealing with difficulties. An affiliated site, www.SparkTop.org for kids ages eight to twelve with learning difficulties—has games, activities, information, opportunities to showcase their strengths.

LD On-Line
National Web site on Learning Disabilities
www.ldonline.org

NON-VERBAL LEARNING DISORDERS

Non-Verbal Learning Disorders Association
www.nlda.org

NLD on the Web
www.nldontheweb.org

SLEEP DISORDERS

American Academy of Sleep Medicine
www.aasmnet.org

American Sleep Disorders Association
www.asda.org

TOURETTE SYNDROME

Tourette Syndrome Association
http://tsa-usa.org